CHOCOLATE
every day

CHOCOLATE
every day

85+ plant-based recipes for cacao treats that support your health and well-being

Not Your Sugar Mamas

Bennett Coffey + Kyleen Keenan

Martha's Vineyard's Favorite Chocolatiers

with Rebecca Miller Ffrench

—

Photography by Elizabeth Cecil

AVERY

an imprint of Penguin Random House

New York

AVERY
an imprint of
Penguin Random House LLC
375 Hudson Street
New York, New York 10014

Most Avery books are available at special quantity discounts for bulk purchase for sales promotions,
premiums, fund-raising, and educational needs. Special books or book excerpts also can be created
to fit specific needs. For details, write SpecialMarkets@penguinrandomhouse.com.

ISBN 9780735216044
ebook ISBN 9780735216051

Printed in the United States of America
10 9 8 7 6 5 4 3 2 1

Book design by Ashley Tucker

This book is dedicated to our devoted fans,
the island community of Martha's Vineyard, and
anyone who needs a little more chocolate in their life

contents

introduction page 9
Why Chocolate? • Our Mission • Our Story

1 all about chocolate page 15
A Health-Supportive Superfood • Chocolate 101

2 getting started with cacao page 23
Keepin' It Simple • Sourcing Raw Chocolate
Ingredients and Such • No Fancy Kitchen Equipment Needed (We Swear!)

3 cacao kitchen essentials page 33

4 cacao drinks and elixirs page 49

5 morning snacks page 73

6 raw candies and treats page 97

7 raw desserts page 129

8 baked goods page 145

9 frozen goodness page 193

Acknowledgments page 216 • Notes page 217 • Index page 218

introduction

One of the most common questions we're asked is "Do you really eat chocolate every day?" The answer: a resounding YES! We're not talking about the mass consumption of highly processed milk chocolate—we all know typical candy bars are often filled with crappy chemical fillers. Instead, we're supporting the mindful incorporation of luxuriously rich and delicious raw cacao into your diet—and yes, every day! Cacao in its raw form is a health food. Period.

If you don't already, we want you to consider cacao in this light. We want to reframe chocolate so you can enjoy it the same healthful way we do. It has been more than twenty years since medical journals first claimed the potential health benefits of chocolate, and the supporting research only continues to grow.[1] Cacao beans are known to contain a large amount of flavonoids, which are antioxidants linked to possible cardiovascular health benefits. Flavonoids have also been found to contain anti-viral, anti-inflammatory, and anti-carcinogenetic properties.[2] Typically, though, cacao beans are roasted at very high temperatures, which has been shown to destroy the flavonoids and reduce the antioxidant levels of the beans.[3]

Additionally most chocolate companies blend their roasted cocoa powder with bleached white sugars, dairy fats, emulsifiers such as soy lecithin, and processed fats like lactose and palm oils, which further negate any of the potential benefits of cacao. The end result is so far removed from the cacao bean that it's hardly chocolate and essentially just a sugary treat!

Unfortunately this means most processed cocoa and the products that contain it are unreliable sources for health benefits. Don't be disheartened, though. Chocolate *can* be made in a different way! We take cacao in its raw, antioxidant-rich form, add organic natural sweeteners and nutrient-rich fats, and turn these ingredients into some of the most delectable treats ever, many of which mimic those commercial candy bars we once loved. We are talking about addictively delicious (in only the best way!) *and* nutritious chocolate foods in many forms.

While our recipes are dairy-, gluten-, and egg-free, we don't subscribe to any one way of eating. Two key factors we feel contribute greatly to a health-supportive diet are eating foods closest to their natural forms and following your body's cues. If you're tired after eating white sugar, avoid it. If gluten makes your tummy hurt, steer clear. We have experienced firsthand that changing the way we eat, if only one whole-foods sweet treat at a time, has greatly affected our overall well-being. Eating chocolate this way, raw and combined with whole-food ingredients, makes us feel more vibrant and alive—and we want you to feel the same.

In the end, the most important thing to us is happiness. If something is healthy for you but doesn't taste good, it won't satisfy you. So we've worked hard over the years to create tasty foods that will doubly satisfy our cravings, both nutritionally and psychologically. Our storefront has served as our testing ground. If folks come back for more, we know we're making something worthwhile. In these pages we share those treasured recipes for delicious treats and customer favorites.

When we say these recipes can be enjoyed without guilt, we really mean it! They're rich from good fats and other nutrients, so a little bit should satisfy you—and go a long way. We hope you find recipes in this book that become your everyday favorites, foods that fuel you in a way that make your days great.

OUR MISSION

We believe that connecting to our highest vibration is one of the most important things we can do at this point in time. The ancient Greeks, after all, introduced us to the idea that everything is energy. Think about it like this: Every little thing on this planet contains some amount of energy within it—from a chair to a person, there is energy in each and every thing. But some things contain more energy than others.

In regards to food, some foods contain a higher vibration, or more "life force," than others. For example, kale is fresh out of the earth, it is a leafy green, and it grows up and out, which gives us the same energetic feeling when we consume it. We feel lighter when we eat kale as opposed to a Snickers bar, which has taken natural ingredients like chocolate, dairy, and nuts and processed them so much that there is very little energy left in the food. In fact, if you consider the nutritional value, Snickers is hardly a food at all, and in the long run, after we eat one we feel sluggish and tired. We are brought down by the lack of energy in that candy bar.

On the other hand, when we are aligned with our higher vibration, we are able to see and think more clearly. We experience more positive, powerful thoughts and can attract positive things to ourselves. When we are on that higher level, we have more energy, feel inspired, and are happier.

We find that when we treat our bodies with love and respect—feed them high-quality foods, exercise, meditate—good things happen. We have the ability to make this choice.

Okay, but what does this have to do with Not Your Sugar Mamas (NYSM)? The intention behind starting NYSM is all of this. The idea is to put a really high-quality, nutrient-dense chocolate bar on the shelves that is also infused with good vibes to make you feel good. We believe that the energy from food infused with good vibes will actually transfer to the person eating it, and will help, even if in a really small way, to raise the vibration of that person. We try to impart this in how we do business: in the relationships we have with each other, with our employees, and with our community, both locally and globally.

When we say we are "spreading the love one kickass chocolate bar at a time," we are not kidding. We believe that by putting superfoods into your body we are helping to shift the vibration. If you're looking to raise your vibrations, we want you to try doing it with chocolate.

We strongly believe chocolate is a vehicle for spreading health and happiness. Because of chocolate's inherent deliciousness, we feel it can help people eat fewer processed foods. It is with this cookbook we show you how.

OUR STORY   Our shared chocolate love started with a joint belief in the power of food. We both traveled extensively before our paths crossed in Martha's Vineyard, and it is those times that greatly influenced our relationship with food. Ky spent some years abroad in Barcelona studying and then later in Argentina, traveling and working. She was greatly inspired by the food and culture and in her free time, she shopped at farmer's markets, cooking up whole foods with abandon and exploring different dietary practices. She also gained firsthand insight into a gluten-free diet due to her roommate's celiac disease. Meanwhile Bennett had a couple of stints in Hawaii and Charleston, which spawned a dedicated yoga practice that inspired a heightened interest in nutrition. She then spent a year studying nutrition before landing back in Martha's Vineyard, where she summered as a child.

During her studies, Bennett was introduced to the idea of raw chocolate, which helped her heal her own addiction to processed sugar. This prompted Bennett to experiment in the kitchen with this irresistible superfood because she wanted to share her breakthrough with others. At the same time, Ky was returning to the Vineyard (she had worked many a summer there) after her time away. She was in pursuit of a more holistic lifestyle after spending too much time stagnant behind a desk, depending on caffeine and sugar to fuel her. There's no other way to say it: She felt like crap. Ky was at a crossroads—she knew it was time for change.

And the start of that change? No joke—Bennett's cacao treats. She felt so satiated and happy from Bennett's chocolate creations she ate after every meal. Because she was feeling better, Ky noticed she was making better food choices throughout the day. It was this small switch over to raw chocolate desserts that made a big difference in Ky's well-being. She also dropped ten pounds without a blink.

We knew Bennett was on to something good, and that's how our journey together toward a more holistic lifestyle began. Not with green juice or salad—but chocolate. Fueled by Ky's business acumen, Bennett's kitchen savvy, and our newfound love for cacao, we plowed ahead. After much dreaming about names, ideas, possibilities, we committed to each other, and to becoming Not Your Sugar Mamas. We felt like we were just dabbling, though. We both had jobs to keep us afloat. It was after we got off-island orders that we knew NYSM was no longer just a hobby. We needed a commercial kitchen.

Shortly after, we rented a storefront on Beach Road in Vineyard Haven Harbor. When we signed the lease, we barely had money to cover the security deposit. We knew we had better start selling chocolate, and fast! We developed more products and grew our business.

The more we learned about the nutritive properties of cacao through sourcing and its growers, the more we were hooked. We had no reservations; we could actually eat chocolate every day.

Are you already wishing you ate cacao daily? Join the club! We're about to show you how you can include cacao in an array of foods, from smoothies to muffins to cakes. Get ready; chocolate can be life changing.

all about chocolate

Antioxidant Power We are proponents of raw chocolate for one simple reason: antioxidants. Cacao is one of the highest antioxidant foods on the planet.[1] It naturally has more antioxidant molecules to inhibit the oxidation of cells. When cells oxidize they lose an electron and become free radicals, which steal electrons from other healthy cells, causing those cells to break down. Antioxidants are like little superheroes streaming through our blood, fighting those electron-stealing free radicals by either donating their own electrons to neutralize them or getting them out of the body.

A Natural Antidepressant

Alkaloids (i.e., cocaine, morphine, etc.) are organic compounds that naturally occur in about 10 percent of the world's plants. Chocolate contains two familiar alkaloids: caffeine and theobromine. Despite what many think, dark chocolate does not have high amounts of caffeine. In fact a 3½-ounce dark chocolate bar has no more caffeine than a cup of coffee. Caffeine is a mood stimulant, as is theobromine. Theobromine stimulates the nervous system, relaxes muscles, and dilates blood vessels. It's also a mild diuretic and cardiac stimulant.

Another mood-boosting benefit of cacao comes through an essential amino acid it delivers called tryptophan (it's "essential" because your body can't produce it, it must be ingested), which is key to serotonin production. The chemical serotonin is credited with promoting positive feelings, mood balance, and spreading love. We mean it! With a large portion of the population on antidepressants, we need more natural and organic ways to improve our moods, and getting the right nutrients is a step in that direction.

A Mineral Booster

Compared to other foods, cacao has one of the highest levels of magnesium. This is likely one of the reasons women tend to crave chocolate during their menstrual cycles: Magnesium helps to relieve cramping. It balances brain chemistry, builds strong bones, keeps blood circulating, and is linked with happier moods. Magnesium also increases the overall vigor of the heart muscle by decreasing blood coagulation, which lowers blood pressure and helps the heart pump more efficiently. Magnesium is one of the most deficient minerals in the standard US diet, with about 48 percent of Americans having chronically deficient magnesium levels.

An Aphrodisiac

If any one food can change your mood, it's chocolate! Phenylethylamine (PEA) is an adrenal-related substance in cacao that's created in the brain and released when we are in love. This is one of the reasons why chocolate and love have a deep correlation. Think chocolates on Valentine's Day.

A Bliss Chemical

Cacao is one of the only plant sources of anandamide, a neurotransmitter that has been isolated in cacao. It's produced naturally in the brain and is known as the bliss chemical because it is released when we are feeling great. Raw cacao is one of the only known sources of anandamide.

An Age Defier and Appetite Suppressant

MAO (Monoamine oxidase) inhibitors may allow more serotonin and other neurotransmitters such as anandamide and dopamine to circulate in the brain. According to author and holistic practitioner Dr. Gabriel Cousens, MAO inhibitors facilitate youthening and rejuvenation, which we can attest to from experience. We are constantly getting comments about having "glowing skin," which neither of us ever got prior to consuming cacao in the way we do now.

MAO inhibitors can also diminish appetite so you feel better *and* look better! Win, win.

CHOCOLATE 101

A Brief History But how do all those amazing nutritive properties go from bean to bar? Cacao grows almost exclusively in the tropical belt, which is the region twenty degrees north and south of the equator. Cacao is grown in thirty-some countries today. The biggest producer is the Ivory Coast, which supplies nearly 30 percent of the world's chocolate. If you add Ghana, Cameroon, and Nigeria to the list, these four West African countries produce a whopping 70 percent of the world's cacao.

Although today much cacao comes from Africa, its origins are deeply rooted in Central and South America. Historians say that the cultures indigenous to these areas consumed cacao seeds as far back as 1900 BC, and cacao was considered a commodity in pre-Columbian Mesoamerica. The ancient Maya mixed ground cacao seeds with honey, vanilla, flowers, chilies, spices, and water to make a bitter, chocolate-flavored drink that in no way resembles the sweetened hot cocoa we are familiar with today. Eventually the Spanish got a hold of this highly valued food and brought it to Europe. There they added sugar to the drink, and by the late seventeenth century, sweetened chocolate drinks were being consumed across the continent.

In 1828 a Dutchman named Coenraad Van Houten changed the way chocolate drinks were made. Before his innovation the chocolate paste used to make drinks gave them a coarse, crumbly texture. Van Houten invented a machine that pressed the chocolate paste and separated the cocoa butter from the cocoa solids. The cocoa solids could then be pulverized to a powder, which, when used, gave drinks a much smoother consistency. Although Van Houten was trying with this process to remove the excess fat and make the chocolate drinks of the time less oily, ironically his discovery paved the way to the creamy chocolate we know today. In the late 1800s Swiss confectioner Daniel Peter began mixing cacao with dairy (dried milk powder from Henri Nestlé, to be exact). Soon after, sugar, milk powders, and other additions were regularly blended with chocolate. This has evolved over time to include artificial sweeteners, lecithins, stabilizers, corn syrups, and other potentially harmful ingredients. As these additions became the norm, we slowly moved farther and farther away from chocolate as a pure food.

An Agricultural Crop

Chocolate may not be the first thing you think of if you're asked to name an agricultural crop. However, about five million farmers in the tropics depend on delicate cacao trees for their livelihoods. As with other crops, the demand for chocolate is rising, so farmers feel they need to increase their yields, begging questions of fair trade, labor conditions, and fertilizer use to boost production. Similar to other farmers today, cacao growers face increasing challenges due to shifting weather patterns and lack of biodiversity caused by deforestation.

We like to compare chocolate to wine. A particular vintage is (usually) made of grapes from a single year. The quality and characteristics of that wine are dependent on the growing conditions of that year—the weather affects the grapes, which in turn affects the final product. The same can be said of cacao beans. We get cacao in its purest form. The beans are not manipulated in a factory to taste the same every single time; instead the taste of our chocolate bars can vary from crop to crop.

Bean to Bar

So how do those little bitter beans become glossy, beautiful brown bars? It all begins with cacao trees, which, once planted, can take up to five years to produce pods (the fruit of the tree). There are three types of cacao trees: the *criollo*, the *forastero*, and the *trinitario*. The criollo is a heritage tree that yields about 5 percent of the world's cacao. We prefer beans from Peruvian criollo trees, which have the most depth of flavor. The forastero tree is much heartier than the criollo, but unfortunately the beans aren't as aromatic, which can result in a lower-quality product. The trinitario is a hybrid of the criollo and forastero trees and combines the characteristics of the two varieties with both hardiness and good flavor. However, the quality of the beans varies depending on the trees from which they were cross-pollinated.

Conventional beans from forastero trees can taste extremely bitter when eaten raw, which is why we like high-quality criollo beans from Peru, which have complex flavors and do not need to be roasted to be palatable. We also prefer cacao powder made from cold-pressed criollo beans.

Farmers spend years closely monitoring young cacao trees before they produce their first crop of beans. The trees are tall—they can grow to be about twenty feet—and unlike a lot of contemporary crops, cacao cannot be harvested by machines. When the pods are ripe, they are cut from the branches and trunks by hand and carefully removed so as not to damage the cocoa flowers or other unripened fruit.

After the pods are harvested, they are broken open and the seeds (beans) are removed. (Note that we use the words "seed" and "bean" interchangeably.) There may be anywhere from twenty to fifty beans per pod, depending on the variety of the tree. The color, size, and shape of the actual pod varies depending on the type of tree, as well.

When the pods are opened, nice clean seeds don't just fall out. Rather, they are enveloped in a sweet, white, almost slimy pulp. The raw seeds are bitter and certainly don't have the luscious aroma we associate with chocolate. The beans, pulp and all,

are put into big wooden boxes—or are sometimes piled between banana leaves or big sacks—and left for five to seven days to ferment. As the heat rises within the containers to a temperature near 115 to 120 degrees Fahrenheit, the pulp becomes liquidy and drains away. While this is happening, complex chemical changes, including oxidation and enzyme activity, occur within the beans. It's this fermentation process that causes the beans to develop the rich flavors we know as chocolate.

After the fermentation process, the beans are dried in the sun or in sheds. Next, the dried beans are sent to factories, where they are sifted and traditionally roasted at high temperatures, which loosens the husk from the bean. The beans then undergo a process called winnowing that separates out the husks, which are used sometimes for fertilizer or can be brewed for tea. Although winnowing is usually done by machine, it can also be done by hand. The husks are removed, and the remaining nibs are ground or pressed into a paste called chocolate liquor (although there's no alcohol in it!).

At this point, the liquor can be used or it can be separated further by removing the fat, or cocoa butter, from the cocoa solids (remember the process Van Houten discovered?). The solids can then be ground to make cocoa powder.

Ironically the cocoa butter and cocoa solids are often blended back together, usually with sweeteners and dairy products, to make chocolate products. Also note, cacao nibs, what remains after the beans have been husked, can also be eaten (raw or roasted) instead of pressed. They have a crunchy texture and are a great nutrient-dense topping for smoothies.

Pure cocoa powder has no extraneous fats or other additives to compromise its flavor or nutrition. It's the essence of chocolate. Cocoa powders typically come in "natural" or "Dutched" varieties. Natural cocoa powder is somewhat acidic, with a pH of 5 to 6 (water has a pH of 7). Dutching is a process that washes the cocoa powder in a potassium carbonate solution to neutralize its pH to 7. Dutched cocoa is darker in color and mellower in flavor, but the process also decreases the nutritive properties of the chocolate. Some recipe writers specifically call for Dutched cocoa because the acidity of natural cocoa powder can react with chemical leaveners to produce carbon dioxide. Although it is disputed how much Dutching compromises cacao's antioxidant value, we always choose raw non-Dutched cacao.

Cacao Versus Cocoa
The use of "cacao" can get fuzzy because people use it interchangeably with "cocoa." For our purposes, we use the word "cacao" when referring to products made with

raw, unroasted beans, and "cocoa" to describe products, including powders, made with processed beans. For example: Cacao butter is the fat that is pressed out of raw, cold-processed cacao beans, while cocoa butter is the fat that is extracted after the beans are processed at high temperatures.

There is much debate surrounding raw cacao versus cocoa because some raw foods advocates argue that even though raw cacao beans are not roasted, they are still fermented and exposed to somewhat hot temperatures. We find that it's the fermentation process (which is natural) that makes the beans delicious and chocolatey. In the end that's what we're really after—a delectable taste—and we're happy to know it comes with health-supportive benefits!

getting started with cacao

We believe that when you use the best ingredients, simple preparation is all you need to make something truly delicious. We are not fans of doing dishes (is anyone?), so with all our recipes, we make the cooking process as easy as possible and aim for the high notes of the chocolate flavor to shine through. You'll also notice that none of the recipes in this book require tempering.

We also never want you to stress about ingredients. We substitute in our own kitchens a lot, and you should feel free to do the same. If we don't have oat milk, we'll use almond. When we're out of cashew butter, we'll sub in sunflower butter. Play around and make these recipes your own. We're conscious of the commitment you'll be making to our recipes, perhaps investing in raw cacao powder or cacao butter for the first time, and because of that we've kept our recipe yields small, often to just two to four servings. We don't want you to make four dozen cookies that you feel obligated to eat! And if you're not dealing with massive amounts of ingredients, it makes things easier on your wallet.

Tempering is a process used to heat and cool chocolate so that it stays solid at room temperature and ensures a smooth, glossy finish with a nice "snap" when you break or bite into it. Chocolate that's melted improperly (not tempered) becomes mottled and doesn't harden well. We could get very scientific and talk about the alignment of molecules and fat crystals but instead we're going to show you it's not necessary to temper chocolate to enjoy it. We weren't kidding when we said we want things easy!

SOURCING RAW CHOCOLATE

Cacao (in all its forms!) When shopping for cacao products, look for those that are unroasted or labeled "raw." You can find cacao in the forms of chips, butter, powder, and nibs, just to name a few. We are big fans of the brand Navitas Organics and you can always order raw cacao products through our website.

We feel very strongly that raw cacao powder is superior because of its higher antioxidant content. That said, natural unsweetened cocoa powder is actually very similar to cacao powder, and while it isn't *bad* for you, it isn't as good for you as cacao powder because it's been processed at much higher temperatures. So when seeking out chocolate, why not just go for the best?

While baking with it may reduce some of its beneficial qualities, we believe starting with a more nutrient-dense product is better, especially because roasted cacao powder does not have any of the additives found in more processed chocolate products. Besides, who can resist baked chocolate confections? When cacao is paired with the right ingredients, you get wonderfully delicious and nutritious treats that can still have healthful benefits.

Steer Clear of Dairy

We're proponents of dairy-free chocolate treats.

As we've mentioned, cacao itself has a very bitter flavor, which is why people traditionally add dairy and sugar to make it creamy and sweet. Unfortunately this might negate its nutritional value. Research shows that when cacao and other high-antioxidant food sources are consumed with milk protein, they may actually lose their antioxidant power. We instead blend cacao with nut and seed butters to impart the creamy, smooth quality we know and love in traditional chocolates. When made this way, the integrity of the original cacao bean is held intact. Read the ingredient labels on your chocolate bars to see if dairy has been added.

Seek Out Natural Sweeteners

Not all sweeteners are created equally. White sugar is a highly processed sweetener. Sugarcane or sugar beets are mashed, and their juices are mixed with chemicals such as lime and phosphoric acid and boiled. The juices are then filtered and whitened using even more chemicals. After the water evaporates, you're left with pure white sugar. The refining process removes nutrients and fiber, meaning that there's nothing to slow down the rate your body absorbs the sugar once it enters your bloodstream. This can send your insulin levels through the roof. And since the sugar has no nutritional value left, your body has to pull from its own reserves of vitamins and minerals to break it down.

Research has shown that consuming a high-sugar diet can tamper with our ability to absorb vitamins C and D, calcium, and magnesium. Spikes in insulin can also use up our supply of zinc and potassium. Simply put, the body has to work extra hard to digest white sugar, depleting other sources of vitamins and minerals just to process it.

On the other hand, natural sweeteners like maple syrup, coconut nectar, honey, and coconut palm sugar are relatively unprocessed and still retain some nutritional value. Maple syrup is made from sap that is boiled down to a syrup. Coconut nectar is another natural sweetener and actually comes from tapping the thick stem of the flowering coconut blossom. We especially like the Coconut Secret brand. Although these syrups are quite concentrated, they still contain trace nutrients and are known for entering the bloodstream at a slower rate than conventional refined white sugar.

We demand a lot from our bodies and if we don't take care of them, we end up feeling exhausted, depleted, and eventually sick. Because of this, it is extremely important to maximize nutrition at any given opportunity, which is why we use only natural sweeteners in our recipes.

While the following list isn't comprehensive, we also try to avoid sucrose, corn syrup, high fructose corn syrup, corn sweetener, and lactose (sugar that comes from milk). If you eat processed foods, as most Americans do, you're likely ingesting these sugars. Even jarred pasta sauce, salad dressing, and ketchup can be loaded with hidden added sugars. You may find that when you eat less sugar, your palate shifts to favor less sweetened foods, which can be completely empowering!

Avoid Anything Artificial

The only sweeteners we deem sketchier than white sugar are artificial varieties like aspartame, saccharin, and sucralose. Research shows that they'll not only disrupt your insulin levels but they'll also negatively impact your microflora—the healthy bacteria found in your gut—which increases your risk of developing obesity and diabetes. Artificial sweeteners are added to millions of food products, including gum, soda, chocolate, and savory foods. Our philosophy is that if you can't pronounce an ingredient, you probably shouldn't eat it. Stick to the natural stuff.

Keep Things Gluten-Free

Because we keep a certified gluten-free kitchen to accommodate customers with strict dietary needs, every recipe in our book is also gluten-free. Although there are many great gluten-free flour mixes on the market today, we prefer to use simple unrefined flours like oat, almond, coconut, and chickpea because they're made from whole ground foods and are naturally nutrient dense. They aren't necessarily interchangeable, so it's best to stick with what the recipe calls for unless otherwise noted. Coconut flour, for example, is super dry. It will absorb much more liquid than most other flours, so if you substituted almond flour, for example, the recipe would turn out entirely different.

And What About Fats?

Healthy fat is vital to our bodies feeling satiated, and it helps build healthy cells that maintain healthy brain and nerve function. Fat also helps curb sugar addictions. Omega-3 and omega-6 fatty acids are important to know because they are essential components of healthy fats. Cacao butter contains several types of fats, including oleic acid, palmitic acid, and stearic acid. Oleic acid is an omega-9 fatty acid, which is the same healthy fat found in olives and avocados and can help raise your HDL, or good cholesterol. Palmitic acid has mild antioxidant and anti-atherosclerotic properties. While stearic acid is a saturated fat, it does not cause cholesterol levels to rise and is considered neutral. Cacao butter also contains a small amount of linoleic acid, another essential omega-6 fatty acid.

When this stable fat is added back to chocolate, it causes it to firm up at room temperature. It keeps the chocolate from spoiling and adds the rich, buttery, melt-in-your-mouth flavor so many of us love. We are also very fond of using coconut oil in our chocolate, for its delicious tropical flavor.

When seeking out chocolate products, the ingredients list tells all. It's surprising that well-known companies still use trans fats in their chocolates. Just take a look at the labels and you'll see.

Deciphering Chocolate Certifications and Labels

We take certifications seriously. We know we're impacting our own health with the foods we purchase and produce, but we're also making political choices and statements with our purchasing power. We attribute much to Craig Sams and Jo Fairley, founders of the Green & Black's chocolate brand, who brought awareness to "ethically correct" chocolate products more than twenty years ago, before such designations existed.

A fair trade certification is given by third-party companies that follow products from source to sale. These parties work to protect farmers by educating them about sustainable production and contributing to community development. All participants are guaranteed a predetermined fair trade price. This protects growers from being paid near-slave wages and ensures that the cacao is being produced without the use of forced labor and that the facilities meet set child labor standards.

A direct trade certification ensures that producers buy directly from the source, which allows more profits to go directly to the farmers. We believe wholeheartedly in buying locally (our community supports us beyond belief!), but there are certain foods that will never be local to the Northeast, such as tea, coffee, and cacao, which require tropical growing conditions. Unlike large, industrialized crops, 80 to 90 percent of cacao comes from small, family-run farms. In some cases middlemen buy beans from the growers and pay pennies on the dollar before selling them to larger companies.

When choosing ingredients, one of the qualities we value most is organic. You are likely familiar with the green or black USDA Organic seal, the round logo that certifies products meet the National Organic Program's (NOP) strict regulations. Per the US Department of Agriculture, the USDA organic seal verifies that a product has 95 percent or more certified organic content. If the label claims that it was made with specified organic ingredients, you can be sure that those specific ingredients are certified organic.

To obtain this label, farms and processing facilities are inspected, records must be submitted, and soil and water are periodically tested, among other practices.

Although you may not associate wheat with chocolate bars, believe it or not, some chocolate products contain gluten. While cacao doesn't inherently contain gluten, ingredients such as malt, malt extract, and malt syrup, which are derivatives of barley, are sometimes added to chocolates. Per the FDA, for a product to be labeled "gluten-free" it must not contain an ingredient that is "1) a gluten-containing grain (e.g., spelt wheat); 2) derived from a gluten-containing grain that has not been processed to remove gluten (e.g., wheat flour); or 3) derived from a gluten-containing grain that has been processed to remove gluten (e.g., wheat starch), if the use of that ingredient results in the presence of 20 parts per million (ppm) or more gluten in the food. Also, any unavoidable presence of gluten in the food must be less than 20 ppm."[1]

Remember, though, these labels are not the only thing to look for when choosing chocolate. The ingredients list is just as important, if not more so. We make it a practice to avoid anything with preservatives. We look for foods with short lists of ingredients that we can pronounce, ensuring we know every one. If you're looking to gain as many health benefits as possible, chocolate or cacao should always be the first ingredient, not sugar or dairy (if sugar is the first ingredient on a chocolate bar, that bar contains more sugar than chocolate!).

Cacao produced to meet these high standards, as you can imagine, requires responsible practices that are more costly than less sustainable methods. In a nutshell: High quality costs more. If you think of purchasing superior-quality chocolate as an investment in your health, though, it makes it more palatable (figuratively and literally!).

INGREDIENTS AND SUCH

"Superfoods" is a term we love because it applies to many of the nutrient-rich foods we use, but unfortunately it's also terribly overused. Marketers have a way of adding this word to the packaging of many foods, some of which may contain a superfood, but in addition to lots of other junk, too. We like to think of superfoods as the really good stuff. Foods that are whole and pure. However, these best-quality foods come with high price tags. We know that almost nine dollars (gasp) for a pound of cassava flour is a lot of dinero, but it's not meant to be consumed in huge quantities. Our recipes are about quality, not quantity.

Because consumers care about their food now more than ever, it's getting easier to source a variety of high-quality ingredients. Health food stores and Whole Foods stores nationwide carry many of the brands we use. Online retailers are a good option for cost-effective sourcing if you live in a rural area.

When stocking your pantry, keep in mind that whole, unprocessed ingredients are key. We don't like to use empty-calorie foods that are devoid of nutrients in anything we do. Our goal is to nourish and satiate with every ingredient.

We're not going to repeat the word "organic" throughout the book, because for us it's a given. We buy organic whenever possible. Not only do we believe organic products are nutritionally superior, we think they contribute to a cleaner environment.

If you were to take a look at our kitchen and peek in our pantry and fridge, this is what you'd find:

Raw Cacao in Many Forms raw cacao powder, raw cacao nibs, raw unsweetened cacao baking bars (A handful of recipes throughout the book call for raw dark chocolate, which is a standard vegan dark chocolate bar 72 percent or higher. You can also use our homemade Traditional Raw Chocolate Bar; see page 34.)

Non-Dairy Milks almond milk, cashew milk, full-fat coconut milk, coconut cream

Sweeteners coconut palm sugar, coconut nectar, raw honey, pure maple syrup (look for grade A: dark color, robust taste maple syrup—it's less refined)

Dates An excellent way to naturally sweeten treats and smoothies. We like Medjool dates the best—the fresher the better. They are soft, sweet, and blend easily. If your dates are dry or hard, we recommend soaking them in hot water for ten minutes to soften, then draining them well before using.

Fats and Oils raw cacao butter, unrefined virgin coconut oil, coconut butter, extra-virgin olive oil

Nuts + Seeds peanuts; raw nuts including almonds, cashews, walnuts, macadamia; seeds including sunflower, flax, chia, sesame; tahini. The secret to the success of many of our recipes is nut and seed butters. They contribute a smooth, creamy texture traditionally provided by dairy and eggs, and they provide healthy fats and protein. Plus they have a great shelf life and are easy to keep around. Nut butters mixed with water also make an easy on-the-spot nut milk (page 43).

Gluten-Free Grains and Flours old-fashioned rolled oats, oat flour, almond flour, coconut flour, chickpea flour, cassava flour, arrowroot flour

Unsweetened Shredded Coconut

Himalayan Sea Salt A pure, clean, unprocessed salt packed with essential minerals like calcium, magnesium, and potassium.

Smoked Sea Salt

Ground Turmeric Made from turmeric rhizomes, it contains a compound called curcumin, a phytochemical known for its antioxidant and anti-inflammatory properties.

Maca Powder A superfood native to the Peruvian Andes and made from the root of the maca plant, which resembles a radish. It is highly valued for its ability to increase energy and fertility.

Mesquite Powder From the seeds of the mesquite tree, native to regions in South America, we use it to sweeten or spice up our recipes. It is high in magnesium, potassium, iron, fiber, and calcium.

Spirulina Considered a plant-based complete protein, this blue-green algae usually comes in tablet or powder form. We prefer the latter for easier absorption because pills oftentimes contain unnecessary fillers.

Pure Vanilla Powder and Extract In our experience vanilla adds a level of flavor and complexity to chocolate that is not achieved with any other ingredient. The sweet, flowery flavoring is available in several different forms: whole pods, extract, powdered, sugar, and paste. Our two favorites are pure vanilla powder and pure vanilla extract. Vanilla powder, made from ground vanilla beans, is a good option for raw recipes because the alcohol used to make vanilla extract can sometimes be detected when it's not cooked off. However, both extract and powder result in a delicious end product, so you can use either one in our recipes. They are a 1:1 substitution, which makes life easy because honestly, we usually just use what we have on hand. A variety of vanillas are available online. We are partial to Nielsen-Massey products.

Frozen Fruit strawberries, bananas, blackberries, cherries, mangoes, etc.

NO FANCY KITCHEN EQUIPMENT NEEDED (WE SWEAR!)

We're not kidding when we say you need just a few things to make all the recipes in our book.

Blender This is probably our most-used kitchen appliance. It's helpful in making smoothies, of course, but we also use it to make sauces, spreads, puddings, ice creams, and much more. A high-speed blender such as a Vitamix or Blendtec is best, but a standard blender will work just fine for most recipes. NutriBullet blenders work well, too.

Food Processor Sometimes this kitchen workhorse is better for chopping and mixing than a blender. A blender can get too hot and ruin the consistency of whatever you're making. Don't worry, we will always indicate which appliance to use and when, or if it just doesn't matter.

Chocolate Molds You don't need fancy or expensive polycarbonate or silicone molds to make amazing chocolate treats. You can get creative and use ice cube trays, mini-cupcake pans, mini-cupcake liners, or whatever you have in your kitchen (how about a jar lid?) to create our confections. We're not saying the other molds aren't useful, just not mandatory. But if you find this chocolate-making thing is for you, there are many interesting shapes and styles of molds, including antique ones, that can be fun to try.

Parchment Paper Boy, is it necessary, and it will make your life so much easier. You won't have to worry about scrubbing sheet trays or popping things out of pans when you use this heat-safe, nonstick paper. Parchment is useful for baked and raw recipes alike.

cacao kitchen essentials: bars, spreads, and more

The following staples, including nut milks, flours, and our basic chocolate bars, are a great place to start your chocolate-making adventures. We call for these throughout the book as parts of other recipes, but you can also keep these items in your fridge and use as desired. It never hurts to have a homemade chocolate bar on hand or a jar filled with The Original Chocolate Spread (page 42) to drizzle over ice cream. We're talking instant gratification here.

homemade chocolate bars three ways

Over the years we have developed three base chocolate recipes that are easy to make and equally delicious (although we are slightly partial to the Fudgy Coconut Butter Bar because the addition of coconut butter makes it extra decadent). They all have their place, and you'll see them used throughout the book. We also like to have one on hand at all times for snacking. A little square is all you'll need to feel satisfied.

|||||||||||||||||||||||||||||

traditional raw chocolate bar

MAKES EIGHT 2 X 4-INCH BARS

Our go-to bar, this recipe yields chocolate similar to a standard store-bought raw chocolate bar. Unlike our other two bars, which need to be refrigerated, this traditional version won't melt at room temperature. When you break off a piece, it's a little "snappier" than our other chocolates, too.

1 cup raw cacao butter, coarsely chopped

1 cup raw cacao powder

¼ cup pure maple syrup

1 teaspoon pure vanilla extract or powder

¼ teaspoon sea salt

1. Line a rimmed baking sheet with parchment paper. Set aside.

2. In a small saucepan over low heat, melt the cacao butter, stirring occasionally, about 3 minutes. Remove from the heat and whisk in the cacao powder, maple syrup, vanilla, and salt, whisking the mixture until completely smooth and no clumps remain. Using a rubber spatula, scrape the mixture onto the prepared baking sheet into an 8 x 8-inch square. (You can make the bar any size you desire. Play around with the thickness you like best.) Chill in the refrigerator for 1 hour, or until firm. Cut into pieces as desired. Store in an airtight container at room temperature for up to 1 month.

favorite freezer chocolate bar

MAKES EIGHT 2 X 4-INCH BARS

As the name implies, this is one of our favorite bars. We love the rich coconut taste, and also its softness—it just melts in your mouth

The upside: This is the best choice for frozen recipes, such as our Watermelon and Chocolate Seed Pops (page 215), because it stays soft when chilled. On the flip side, because there is no cacao butter or preservatives like those used in many store-bought bars, this variation melts at room temperature, so it needs to be stored in the refrigerator.

1 cup unrefined virgin coconut oil

1 cup raw cacao powder

¼ cup pure maple syrup

1. Line a rimmed baking sheet with parchment paper. Set aside.

2. In a small saucepan over low heat, melt the coconut oil, stirring occasionally, about 3 minutes. Remove from the heat and whisk in the cacao powder and maple syrup, whisking the mixture until completely smooth and no clumps remain.

3. Using a rubber spatula, scrape the mixture onto the prepared baking sheet and shape it into an 8 x 8-inch square (again, same as the Traditional Bar, you can make this any desired thickness). Chill in the freezer for 30 minutes, or until firm. Store in an airtight container in the refrigerator for up to 1 month.

fudgy coconut butter chocolate bar

MAKES EIGHT 2 X 4-INCH BARS

This bar is even richer than our coconut oil–based Favorite Freezer Chocolate Bar (page 35), The addition of coconut butter, which is a spread made from fibrous coconut shreds, makes this chocolate especially tasty, and denser, with more texture from the coconut meat. Think peanut oil versus peanut butter when comparing coconut oil– and coconut butter–based bars. We like to melt this fudgelike bar to use as a coating for our confections, too.

½ cup raw cacao butter,
    coarsely chopped

½ cup coconut butter

1 cup raw cacao powder

¼ cup pure maple syrup

1. Line a rimmed baking sheet with parchment paper. Set aside.

2. In a small saucepan over low heat, melt the cacao and coconut butters, stirring occasionally, about 3 minutes. Remove from the heat and whisk in the cacao powder and maple syrup until completely smooth and no clumps remain.

3. Using a rubber spatula, scrape the mixture onto the prepared baking sheet into an 8 x 8-inch square (as with the Traditional Bar, you can make this any desired thickness). Chill in the refrigerator for 30 minutes, or until firm. Store in an airtight container in the refrigerator for up to 1 month.

prep note • When making chocolate bars with our methods, use liquid sweeteners. Powdered ones tend to settle at the bottom of the mixture and make the end product gritty.

chocolate magic shell

MAKES ABOUT ½ CUP

We don't know what we love more about this sauce: how it tastes or how much fun it is to crack with a spoon when it hardens. The secret behind the magic is coconut oil, which firms up immediately when it's chilled. Be sure whatever you're pouring the sauce on, like ice cream or sorbet, is frozen, or at least as cold as possible, so the magic really does happen.

¼ cup unrefined virgin coconut oil

¼ cup raw cacao powder

¼ cup pure maple syrup, agave nectar, or raw honey

Melt the coconut oil in a small saucepan over low heat. Whisk in the cacao powder and maple syrup until the mixture is smooth and no lumps remain. Continue to cook until bubbles just begin to appear. Allow the mixture to cool slightly before using. If the chocolate hardens, you can heat it again to make it pourable. Store in a jar or covered container in the refrigerator for up to 3 weeks.

be saucy chocolate sauce

MAKES ABOUT 1¼ CUPS

Drizzle this chocolate sauce on anything and everything, from our Black and White Frappe (page 194) to our Brownie Trifle with Caramelized Bananas (page 139).

¾ cup liquid sweetener, such as pure maple syrup or coconut nectar

¾ cup raw cacao powder

In a small saucepan over low heat, combine the sweetener with ¼ cup of water and cook until the mixture just starts to bubble, about 4 minutes. Whisk in the cacao powder until smooth. If desired, pour the heated mixture into a blender or use an immersion blender to puree the sauce until super smooth. Store in a jar or covered container in the refrigerator for up to 1 week. Reheat before using.

homemade chocolate bars,
page 34

almond butter caramel sauce

You can make this caramel sauce as thin or thick as you like by increasing or decreasing the amounts of water and/or almond butter. Drizzle it over ice cream or fruit, or even on a chocolate tart. See photo, page 32.

½ cup coconut nectar

6 tablespoons almond butter

¼ cup unrefined virgin coconut oil, melted

1 teaspoon pure vanilla extract or powder

⅛ teaspoon sea salt

Combine the coconut nectar, almond butter, coconut oil, vanilla, and salt in a food processor or blender and puree until smooth. Add water 1 tablespoon at a time, pureeing between additions, adding up to 6 tablespoons, until you reach your desired consistency. Store in a jar or covered container in the refrigerator for up to 1 month.

coconut caramel sauce

MAKES 1½ CUPS

This caramel sauce holds its shape better than the almond butter version, which makes this a good option for making bars and candies.

One 13.5-ounce can full-fat coconut milk

1 cup coconut palm sugar

1 tablespoon pure vanilla extract or powder

¼ teaspoon sea salt

In a small saucepan over medium heat, combine the coconut milk and coconut palm sugar and bring to a simmer. Cook until the mixture thickens slightly and coats the back of a spoon, about 15 minutes. Stir in the vanilla and salt and allow to cool slightly before using as desired. Store in a jar or covered container in the refrigerator for up to 2 weeks.

prep note • If you want a thicker sauce, like dulce de leche, for example, add ¼ cup of cashew butter with the coconut milk.

the original chocolate spread

MAKES ABOUT 1 CUP

This recipe will always be special to us—it is the original recipe that has inspired all our chocolates. We consider it a chocolate bar you eat with a spoon. After it's cooled, it's similar in consistency to a spread like Nutella and is tasty slathered on toast. While it's still warm after cooking, it works well as a sauce or dip, too. You can always reheat it to make it sauce-like again as well.

½ cup coconut butter

1 cup raw cacao powder

¾ cup pure maple syrup

1 teaspoon ground cinnamon

1 teaspoon pure vanilla extract or powder

½ teaspoon sea salt

1. In a small saucepan melt the coconut butter over low heat, stirring occasionally, about 3 minutes. Remove from the heat and whisk in the cacao powder, maple syrup, cinnamon, vanilla, and salt, whisking the mixture until completely smooth and no clumps remain.

2. Reheat to spread on toast or fruit or pour over your favorite ice cream. Store in a jar or covered container in the refrigerator for up to 1 month.

creamy homemade nut milks

MAKES 1 CUP

Making homemade milk greatly expands your dairy-free options and guarantees you a fresh, preservative-free product with a wallet-friendly price tag. We give two methods here. If you have a high-speed blender such as a Vitamix or Blendtec, both methods will work well. If you have a standard blender, we recommend Option 1.

OPTION 1:

Are you ready for our favorite hack? The best secret ever?

Just blend 1 heaping tablespoon nut butter or coconut butter with 1 cup water and voilà, you have nut milk!

OPTION 2:

In a high-speed blender, combine ¼ cup raw cashews, raw macadamia nuts, or blanched almonds with 1 cup of water and 1 to 2 dates and process on high until completely smooth. Note: Soak the nuts in hot water for 10 minutes before blending.

soaking nuts

To soak or not to soak? We like to soak our nuts when we have the time. Not only do they blend more easily, but soaking also reduces phytic acid. Phytic acid occurs naturally in nuts and can bind with minerals, which may prevent the minerals from being absorbed by our bodies. To soak, simply add the nuts to a bowl or container, cover with water, allow them to sit for at least 8 hours or overnight, and then drain and rinse them before using. We'll let you know if a recipe requires pre-soaked nuts, but otherwise, soak at your own discretion.

coconut whipped cream

MAKES ABOUT 1 CUP

Coconut whipped cream is one of our favorite ways to finish off our desserts. We always keep a can of coconut milk on hand in the refrigerator so we can whip up a batch at a moment's notice. We recommend you avoid coconut milk that contains guar gum, an additive that emulsifies the milk and fat. Cans of unsweetened coconut cream are also now available. The cream from a can of coconut milk equals about 8 ounces unsweetened canned coconut cream.

One 13.5-ounce can full-fat coconut milk, chilled overnight (try not to tip or shake the can, as you want the solids to separate from the liquid)

Splash pure vanilla extract

½ cup powdered maple or coconut palm sugar (see Prep Note), or drizzle of pure maple syrup (optional)

1. Gently open the can of coconut milk and transfer the solids that have settled at the top to the bowl of a stand mixer (reserve the liquid for another use) or a medium mixing bowl. Add the vanilla, and if using the sugar, add it now, too.

2. With the whisk attachment or using a hand mixer, beat the coconut cream on medium-high speed until light and fluffy. Use right away or place in the refrigerator and rewhip before using (allow it to soften to room temperature first). Store in an airtight container for up to 1 week.

prep note • To make homemade powdered sugar, place the sugar in a high-speed blender and process until fine (½ cup granulated or coconut sugar yields ½ cup powdered). It won't be as fluffy as traditional confectioners' sugar, but it'll dissolve nicely into the cream. Use the leftover coconut milk for baking or making smoothies.

homemade
nut and grain flours

It's astonishing how easy it is to make your own flours. With a blender or food processor you can have freshly ground flours in minutes. We make almond and oat flours the most, but you can substitute almost any nut or grain.

||||||||||||||||

almond flour
and almond meal

MAKES ABOUT 1 CUP

Almond flour and almond meal are similar ingredients, but there's a key difference: Almond meal is made from whole, unblanched almonds, while almond flour is usually made from blanched almonds and is more finely ground. They are more or less interchangeable unless you're looking to achieve a finer texture, in which case opt for almond flour. Be careful when processing the nuts—an extra second or two and your flour can turn into almond butter!

2 cups blanched or unblanched raw almonds

1. Add the almonds to a blender or food processor and run for 30 to 60 seconds, until the almonds are finely ground into a powder.

2. Store in an airtight container in the refrigerator for up to 2 weeks.

||||||||||||||||

oat flour

MAKES ABOUT 1 CUP

This is an excellent option for gluten-free baking. Be sure your oats are certified gluten-free if gluten is a concern.

1 cup old-fashioned rolled oats

1. Add the oats to a blender or food processor and run for 30 to 60 seconds, until the oats are finely ground.

2. Store in an airtight container at room temperature for up to 1 month.

plant-based egg replacers

These vegan egg replacers are game changers when it comes to egg-free baking. The black chia eggs may affect the color of your final product, so keep that in mind when choosing between the two recipes (white chia seeds are an option as well). Otherwise, they're both excellent binders.

chia eggs

1 egg = 1 tablespoon ground chia seeds plus 2½ tablespoons water

2 eggs = 2 tablespoons ground chia seeds plus 5 tablespoons water

In a small bowl, stir together the chia seeds and water and let sit 5 minutes before using.

flax eggs

1 egg = 1 tablespoon ground flaxseed plus 2½ tablespoons water

2 eggs = 2 tablespoons ground flaxseed plus 5 tablespoons water

In a small bowl, stir together the flaxseed and water and let sit 5 minutes before using.

prep note • Grind chia seeds in a blender, food processor, or spice grinder before measuring.

cacao drinks and elixirs

Cacao was originally enjoyed in beverages, and
liquid chocolate refreshment remains a classic.
Our drinks may have evolved from the
bitter versions of Mesoamerica, but by using
only unroasted cacao and other whole,
high-quality foods, we honor cacao and
its history as an ingredient in sacred elixirs.

everyday chocolate smoothie

SERVES 1

This is how we like to take our cacao in the AM: a smoothie made of sweet cherries, banana, chocolate, and spirulina, a type of alkalizing blue-green algae that's a plant-based complete protein. While a teaspoon of this sea vegetable doesn't really add flavor to the smoothie, it does contribute good nutrition, including iron, calcium, and vitamins A, E, and K. Did we mention this smoothie also tastes like ice cream? Another reason to eat chocolate every day!

½ **frozen banana**

1 **cup frozen sweet cherries**

2 **tablespoons raw cacao powder**

2 **tablespoons cashew, almond, or coconut butter**

1 **teaspoon spirulina**

Optional add-ins: 1 cup fresh spinach, 1 tablespoon chia seeds, 1 teaspoon maca powder, or 1 tablespoon flaxseed

In a blender, combine 1 cup water, banana, cherries, cacao powder, nut butter, spirulina, and your desired add-ins and puree until smooth and creamy. If the blade is struggling, add up to ¼ cup of water to get it running. Serve immediately.

prep note • If you are using a high-speed blender, you can replace the nut butter with ¼ cup of raw cashews if desired.

secret to a successful smoothie

One of our best tips is our method for measuring smoothie ingredients using only your smoothie glass. Use this method for your own favorite blends, or try experimenting with new ones, inspired by cacao and other healthful ingredients. Simply place all your ingredients, including ice, in the glass you're going to drink out of and add enough liquid to fill the glass. At least half the glass should be filled with liquid. For example, in a 16-ounce glass, you want to use about 8 ounces of liquid. Then pour all the ingredients into the blender and puree on high. When you pour the blended drink into the glass, it should fill just to the top and have a smooth, creamy consistency. If you're using frozen fruit, you'll need less ice, as the fruit does double duty, chilling the drink while adding flavor and texture.

   This is also a great way to prep smoothies and shakes. At our cafe, we store the ingredients in cups in the freezer, then we just add liquid and blend.

chocolate malted milkshake

SERVES 1

When Ky was little, her dad would sometimes let her play hooky from school and they'd go grab malted milkshakes from their favorite spot. This version mimics those creamy, cold drinks. Instead of malt powder we add maca powder, a super-food native to the Peruvian Andes. It's the root of the maca plant, which resembles a radish and is highly valued for its ability to increase energy and fertility. If you don't have maca, though, no worries—simply leave it out and you'll still have a delicious chocolate shake!

1 cup ice, plus more as needed

½ cup unsweetened shredded coconut

¼ cup raw cashews

4 pitted dates (about ¼ cup)

2 teaspoons raw cacao powder

1 teaspoon maca powder

Combine the ice, 1 cup water, the coconut, cashews, dates, cacao powder, and maca powder in a high-speed blender and puree until smooth and creamy. Add more ice for a thicker consistency if desired. Serve immediately.

prep note • If you don't have a high-speed blender, use 1 tablespoon of cashew butter and 2 tablespoons of coconut butter in place of the cashews and shredded coconut.

white chocolate smoothie

SERVES 1

This smoothie is our attempt at capturing our white chocolate bar in a glass. Even though the smoothie contains no trace of chocolate at all (cold cacao butter just doesn't blend up well), it still has a creamy white chocolate taste with hints of vanilla and maple. We achieve the rich, delicate flavor that cacao butter lends to white chocolate by using a combination of cashews and coconut oil instead. This refreshing drink, which is thinner than a traditional smoothie, is undoubtedly a customer favorite.

1 cup ice, plus more as needed

¼ cup raw cashews or
  2 tablespoons cashew butter

¼ cup unsweetened shredded coconut

1 tablespoon unrefined virgin coconut oil

1 tablespoon pure maple syrup

¼ teaspoon pure vanilla powder or the seeds scraped from 1 whole vanilla bean

Combine the ice, 1 cup water, the cashews, coconut, coconut oil, maple syrup, and vanilla in a high-speed blender and puree until smooth and creamy. Add more ice for a thicker consistency if desired. Serve immediately.

strawberry chocolate almond butter smoothie

SERVES 1

Do you ever go to bed thinking about what you're going to have for breakfast? Bennett does, and often it's because she's looking forward to drinking this smoothie blend the next morning. The hemp seeds and almond butter add a boost of protein, and the sweet, delicate flavor of strawberries plus the slight bitterness of cacao make this smoothie seem more like a dessert than a nutritious, fiber-filled beverage. Chocolate-covered strawberries, anyone?

1 cup almond milk

½ frozen banana

¾ cup frozen strawberries (about 8 whole)

1 heaping tablespoon raw cacao powder

1 tablespoon raw honey

1 tablespoon almond butter

1 tablespoon hemp seeds

½ teaspoon pure vanilla extract or powder

4 ice cubes

Combine the almond milk, banana, strawberries, cacao powder, honey, almond butter, hemp seeds, and vanilla with the ice in a high-speed blender and puree until smooth and creamy. Serve immediately.

banana date cacao smoothie,
page 58

strawberry chocolate
almond butter smoothie

mint chocolate chip
smoothie,
page 57

mint chocolate chip smoothie

SERVES 1

If you're a fan of mint chocolate chip ice cream, then this blend is for you. Fresh mint is the star, complemented by crunchy cacao nibs. Banana, nuts, and dates play a supporting role, adding sweetness and a creamy texture. A nice amount of spinach adds a good dose of greens as well.

1 cup fresh spinach

1 frozen banana

10 to 12 cashews
(about 2 tablespoons)

2 pitted dates

2 tablespoons packed fresh
mint leaves

1 to 2 tablespoons raw cacao nibs

½ teaspoon pure vanilla extract
or powder

Combine 1½ cups water, the spinach, banana, cashews, dates, mint, 1 tablespoon of cacao nibs, and the vanilla in a high-speed blender and puree on high until smooth and creamy. For a chocolate chip–like crunch, stir another tablespoon of nibs into your glass after blending. Serve immediately.

banana date cacao smoothie

SERVES 1

This smoothie's name is slightly misleading. While it contains banana and dates, it tastes like a refreshing glass of chocolate milk, but without any of the yucky ingredients often found in premade varieties. Our version has potassium and fiber, and the chia seeds and almond butter will help you feel full longer. We spice it up with a dash of cinnamon for an added layer of flavor.

1 cup non-dairy milk

Generous handful ice cubes

½ frozen banana

2 pitted dates

1 tablespoon chia seeds

1 tablespoon almond butter

1 tablespoon raw cacao powder

½ teaspoon pure vanilla extract or powder

¼ teaspoon ground cinnamon

Combine the milk, ice, banana, dates, chia seeds, almond butter, cacao powder, vanilla, and cinnamon in a high-speed blender and puree on high until smooth and creamy. Serve immediately.

coffee mocha smoothie

SERVES 1

When Bennett lived in Hawaii, she worked in a vegetarian cafe that served a smoothie similar to this one. Her version uses coffee ice cubes and a generous bit of cacao powder to create a powerful pick-me-up. We also add mesquite powder, which comes from the seeds of a tree native to South America and contains magnesium, potassium, iron, fiber, and calcium. We like the smoky, nutty flavor it lends.

FOR THE CHOCOLATE SAUCE:
- ¼ cup liquid sweetener, such as coconut nectar or pure maple syrup
- ¼ cup raw cacao powder

FOR THE SMOOTHIE:
- 1 cup non-dairy milk
- 4 coffee ice cubes (see Prep Note)
- 1 tablespoon raw cacao powder
- 1 teaspoon mesquite powder (optional)
- 2 or 3 pitted dates
- Handful ice (optional)

1. **Make the chocolate sauce:** Combine the sweetener and cacao powder in a blender and pulse several times until smooth. Add hot water, 1 tablespoon at a time, until the sauce reaches the consistency of honey. Pour the sauce into a small container and set aside. No need to rinse out the blender at this point.

2. **Make the smoothie:** Combine the milk, coffee ice cubes, cacao powder, mesquite powder, and dates in the blender and puree on high until smooth and creamy. Add more ice for a thicker consistency if desired. Pour into a drinking glass and top with the chocolate sauce.

prep note • You can make coffee ice cubes by simply freezing brewed coffee in a standard-size ice cube tray.

summer chocolate horchata

SERVES 4 TO 6

When Ky lived in Spain, she became obsessed with horchata, a creamy iced drink that is traditionally made with white rice, blanched almonds, white sugar, and cinnamon. She even visited its place of origin, Valencia, to learn more about it. Back Stateside, she created a healthier version using brown rice and dates, to help promote digestive health and, of course, a little chocolate for an antioxidant boost.

½ cup brown rice

½ cup blanched almonds

12 pitted dates

1 tablespoon raw cacao powder

1 teaspoon pure vanilla extract
  or powder

Pinch sea salt

1. Combine the rice and almonds in a large bowl and cover with water. Allow to soak overnight or at least 12 hours. Drain and rinse.

2. Add the soaked almonds and rice to a high-speed blender with 3 cups water. Blend on high for 1 to 2 minutes, until smooth. Using a fine-mesh strainer or nut milk bag, strain the liquid into a medium bowl and discard the solids or save them for another use. Pour the strained mixture back into the blender and add the dates, cacao powder, vanilla, and salt. Blend again until smooth and creamy. Serve chilled or over ice. Store in the refrigerator up to 1 week.

mexican chocolate cashew milk

SERVES 1

Warm and comforting, this smooth cashew milk drink is the perfect balance of sweet with a little spice. We like to drink it warm, but it's also delicious served cold—just store it in a mason jar in the fridge.

¼ cup raw cashews

2 pitted dates

2 ounces 72% or darker raw chocolate or Traditional Raw Chocolate Bar (page 34), chopped

1 teaspoon ground cinnamon

1 teaspoon freshly ground nutmeg

1 teaspoon pure vanilla extract or powder

½ teaspoon ground cardamom

Pinch cayenne pepper

① Combine 1¼ cups water, the cashews, and dates in a high-speed blender and puree on high until smooth.

② Pour the cashew mixture into a small saucepan over medium-low heat and cook until it just starts to simmer. Add the chopped chocolate to the saucepan and whisk until melted. Pour the chocolate cashew milk back into the blender and add the cinnamon, nutmeg, vanilla, cardamom, and cayenne. Blend to combine, about 10 seconds. Drink while warm.

be cozy,
page 70

white hot chocolate,
page 66

superfood
hot chocolate,
page 69

white hot chocolate

SERVES 1

Smooth and creamy, this lighter version of cocoa is a must for white chocolate lovers. Not overly sweet, a touch of honey is balanced by a pinch of cinnamon. Cacao butter, a healthy fat, helps rev your metabolism and warms you to the core. Try adding a pinch of cardamom or nutmeg for an additional sweet-spicy twist.

1 cup store-bought or Creamy Homemade Cashew Milk (page 43)

1 tablespoon raw cacao butter

1 tablespoon raw honey

⅛ teaspoon pure vanilla extract or powder

⅛ teaspoon ground cinnamon

Coconut Whipped Cream, for serving (optional; page 44)

Pinch of cardamom or nutmeg (optional)

In a small saucepan over medium-low heat, whisk together the milk, cacao butter, and honey until the butter is melted and incorporated. Transfer the warm milk mixture to a blender and add the vanilla and cinnamon. Blend until frothy. Serve warm and with a dollop of coconut whipped cream and cardamom if desired.

superfood
hot chocolate

SERVES 1

If you're looking to replace your morning coffee, this is the drink to do it with. We added turmeric, ginger, cinnamon, and, of course, a little cacao to bring this spiked hot chocolate to superfood status. There is lots of room for variation, so play with the ingredients and make it your own.

2 tablespoons raw cacao powder

1 tablespoon coconut palm sugar

1½ teaspoons unrefined virgin coconut oil

1 teaspoon ground turmeric

Pinch ground ginger

Pinch ground cinnamon

1 cup non-dairy milk

In a large mug, whisk together the cacao powder, sugar, coconut oil, turmeric, ginger, and cinnamon. Heat the milk in a saucepan over medium heat until it just begins to simmer. Pour it over the hot chocolate mix and whisk until smooth and creamy. Drink warm.

be cozy

SERVES 1

Bennett created this recipe the first winter we were in business, and it remains a cherished cold-weather drink. It features lucuma powder, which is made from an exotic Peruvian fruit that looks somewhat like a mango with an avocado pit and is touted for its antioxidant properties. A spoonful adds a natural, almost maplelike sweetness to this warming cup of cacao.

1 tablespoon raw cacao powder

1 tablespoon coconut palm sugar

1 teaspoon lucuma powder

½ teaspoon ground cinnamon

¼ teaspoon pure vanilla extract or powder

Pinch sea salt

1 cup non-dairy milk

1. In a large mug, whisk together the cacao powder, sugar, lucuma, cinnamon, vanilla, and salt.

2. Heat the milk in a small saucepan over medium heat until it just begins to simmer and pour it over the mix in the mug. Whisk until smooth and creamy. Drink warm.

5

morning snacks

If you're like us, at some point in your life you've
had a bad sugar trip from way-too-sweet nutrition-
deficient breakfast treats. They send you up high
but also bring you down, only to make you grab for
another carb- or caffeine-loaded food. The cycle is
downright debilitating. Happily that is exactly what
you won't get from the recipes in this chapter. These
seemingly decadent morning snacks are filled with
fiber, nutrients, and all the benefits of chocolate—
and its delicious taste—which will power you
through the start of the day with good energy and
NO crashing. Mornings are looking sunnier already!

maple-glazed chocolate doughnuts

MAKES 4 DOUGHNUTS

Bennett loves doughnuts, but for a while, she had (mostly) written them off. She just couldn't justify the processed ingredients or the deep-frying. Until, that is, these healthy baked beauties put her back in the game! They may look sinful with their glossy coconut maple glaze, but they aren't; they're just devilishly delicious. You'll need a nonstick doughnut pan for these.

FOR THE DOUGHNUTS:

2 cups almond flour

½ cup raw cacao powder

½ cup coconut palm sugar

½ cup almond milk

6 tablespoons unrefined virgin coconut oil, melted

2 teaspoons pure vanilla extract or powder

½ teaspoon baking powder

½ teaspoon sea salt

FOR THE GLAZE:

1¾ cups maple sugar

¼ cup coconut cream

1 teaspoon pure vanilla powder

1 teaspoon fresh lemon juice

① Position a rack in the center of the oven and preheat to 350°F.

② **Make the doughnuts:** In a large bowl, stir together the flour, cacao powder, sugar, almond milk, coconut oil, vanilla, baking powder, and salt until well combined. Divide the batter among 4 wells of a nonstick doughnut pan, filling each one about three-quarters full. Bake for 12 to 14 minutes, until the doughnuts spring back when pressed lightly. Let them cool completely in the pan.

③ **While the doughnuts cool, make the glaze:** Add the maple sugar to a high-speed blender or food processor and run on high until a fine powder forms. Add the coconut cream, vanilla, lemon juice, and 2 tablespoons of water. Blend again until smooth.

④ Place the cooled doughnuts on a wire rack set over parchment paper and drizzle evenly with the glaze. Transfer the glazed doughnuts to a plate and refrigerate for about 10 minutes, or until the glaze hardens. These will keep in an airtight container in the refrigerator for up to 1 week.

no-cook chocolate chia oatmeal

SERVES 1

Bennett rarely strays from her morning smoothie routine, but when she does, this delicious bowl of oatmeal is her go-to alternative. We use old-fashioned rolled oats because they're less processed than quick oats. And because we love shortcuts, we don't stand at the stove cooking the oats. We just pour boiling water over them and attend to another morning task. They don't get as soft and fluffy as if they were cooked, but the chia and fruit contribute to a wonderfully satisfying texture. For die-hard chocolate fans, sprinkle on a handful of chopped chocolate to boost the cocoa flavor.

½ cup old-fashioned rolled oats

1 tablespoon black or white chia seeds

3 tablespoons coconut palm sugar, plus more to taste

2 tablespoons raw cacao powder

Generous pinch sea salt

¾ cup boiling water

1 tablespoon almond butter or another nut butter

½ banana, peeled and chopped (optional; see Prep Note)

Seeds of ¼ pomegranate (about ¼ cup; optional—see Prep Note)

½ ounce 72% or darker raw chocolate, chopped (optional)

In a cereal bowl, stir together the oats, chia seeds, sugar, cacao powder, and salt, then pour in the boiling water. Add the almond butter and stir well to combine. Add more coconut sugar if desired. Let the mixture stand for 5 minutes to thicken, then mix in the banana, pomegranate, and chopped chocolate, if using. Serve hot.

prep note • Feel free to replace the banana and pomegranate with any fruit you have—blueberries, strawberries, and pineapple are great options—or leave the fruit out altogether for a chocolate-only treat.

morning power muffins

MAKES 8 MUFFINS

Thinking about all the refined flours and sugars and even hydrogenated oils in your average muffin takes away any pleasure there may be in eating one. We wanted to come up with a fresh morning muffin that left us feeling energized, not weighed down. These power muffins have a rich, luxurious taste, and almost every ingredient packs a nutritional punch: oats help stabilize blood sugar, raw cacao and blueberries supply antioxidants, almond butter and flaxseed provide protein, and bananas give a dose of potassium. Switch it up and top the muffins with whatever you have on hand: We suggest cacao nibs with cinnamon and coconut sugar, walnuts with blueberries, or shredded coconut.

1 cup oat flour

¼ cup almond butter

3 tablespoons raw cacao powder

2 bananas, peeled and coarsely chopped

2 tablespoons pure maple syrup

1 tablespoon flaxseed meal

1 teaspoon pure vanilla extract or powder

½ teaspoon baking soda

¼ teaspoon salt

2 Flax Eggs (page 47)

1 cup fresh blueberries

Shelled walnuts, raw cacao nibs, coconut flakes, coconut sugar, or ground cinnamon, for serving (optional)

1. Position a rack in the center of the oven and preheat to 350°F. Line a standard muffin pan with 8 paper liners. Set aside.

2. In a high-speed blender or food processor, combine ¾ cup of the flour, the almond butter, cacao powder, bananas, maple syrup, flaxseed meal, vanilla, baking soda, and salt. Pulse until smooth. Add the flax eggs and pulse another few times until fully combined. In a medium bowl, toss the blueberries with the remaining ¼ cup of the flour to coat. Scrape the blended mixture into the bowl and use a rubber spatula to gently fold in the blueberries.

3. Spoon the batter into the prepared muffin pan, dividing it evenly among the paper liners. Sprinkle with the toppings of your choice.

④ Bake the muffins for 18 to 20 minutes, until the tops spring back when pressed lightly with your finger and a toothpick comes out with just a few moist crumbs attached. Let the muffins cool for at least 15 minutes in the pan before removing, then allow them to cool completely on a rack before eating.

prep note •

To make fresh sweet potato puree, peel one large sweet potato and cut into chunks. In a small saucepan, cover the potato with water. Bring to a boil, then reduce the heat to a simmer and cook for 20 minutes, or until the potato is tender and pierces easily with a fork. Drain and then puree in a blender or food processor.

zucchini bread
with chocolate sweet potato frosting

MAKES ONE 9 X 5-INCH LOAF

Come summer's end, it seems like everyone on the island is trying to pawn off extra zucchini. Ky remembers her mother baking their zucchini harvest into sweet loaves with a swirly cream cheese frosting, which Ky delivered to friends and neighbors. Here a sweet potato and chocolate frosting updates this childhood favorite, giving the bread an equally creamy finish without dairy or added sugar. The loaf is not too sweet and, left unfrosted, gets deliciously crunchy when toasted.

FOR THE BREAD:

Coconut oil, for greasing the pan

2½ cups old-fashioned rolled oats

2 medium bananas, peeled and mashed (about 1 cup)

1 cup grated zucchini (about 1 small zucchini), squeezed of excess water

½ cup pure maple syrup, agave, or raw honey

⅓ cup unrefined virgin coconut oil

4½ tablespoons apple cider or white vinegar

1½ teaspoons pure vanilla extract or powder

1 teaspoon baking soda

1 teaspoon baking powder

¾ teaspoon sea salt

1 teaspoon ground cinnamon

FOR THE CHOCOLATE SWEET POTATO FROSTING:

¾ cup sweet potato puree, canned or fresh (see Prep Note)

8 ounces 72% or darker raw chocolate, chopped

① Position a rack in the center of the oven and preheat to 350°F. Thoroughly grease a 9 x 5-inch loaf pan with oil and set aside.

② **Make the zucchini bread:** Combine all ingredients in a blender and blend until smooth. Using a spatula, scrape down the sides and run on medium speed for another 15 seconds, or until consistently smooth. Pour the batter into the prepared pan.

③ Bake for 40 minutes, or until a toothpick comes out clean. Cool in the pan for 15 minutes, then turn out onto a rack to cool completely before frosting.

④ **Make the chocolate sweet potato frosting:** In a small saucepan over medium heat, cook the sweet potato puree until it just begins to simmer. Remove from the heat and add the chopped chocolate. Stir vigorously until the chocolate melts and is thoroughly incorporated. Set aside to cool completely. Spread the cooled frosting over the zucchini bread.

chocolatey
orange scones,
page 89

churro waffles,
page 93

no-cook chocolate
chia oatmeal
page 77

chocolate
banana bread,
page 86

chocolate banana bread

MAKES ONE 9 X 5-INCH LOAF

If you buy bananas regularly, like we do, from time to time you'll most likely have a few that turn too ripe to eat. We welcome those overripe brown gems that combine with cacao powder and a few other ingredients to create a simple, delectable loaf. It's so easy to make, you don't even need a mixer; just whisk the dry ingredients, add the wet, stir, and bake. The resulting loaf is extremely moist with an intense cocoa flavor.

Coconut oil, for greasing the pan

2 cups almond flour

⅓ cup raw cacao powder

1 teaspoon baking soda

1 teaspoon baking powder

1½ teaspoons ground cinnamon

½ teaspoon sea salt

3 ripe medium bananas, peeled

2 Flax Eggs (page 47)

¼ cup pure maple syrup

¼ cup almond butter

1 teaspoon pure vanilla extract or powder

prep note • You can
freeze ripe bananas for future use and have them on hand to make this loaf. To freeze, peel and slice bananas into ¼-inch slices and spread them in a single layer on a baking sheet. Freeze uncovered for 2 hours. Transfer to an airtight container or zippered freezer bag and store for up to 2 months.

1. Position a rack in the center of the oven and preheat to 350°F. Thoroughly grease a 9 x 5-inch loaf pan and set aside.

2. In a large bowl, whisk together the flour, cacao powder, baking soda, baking powder, cinnamon, and salt. Set aside.

3. Add the bananas to a separate medium bowl and mash them almost smooth. Add the flax eggs, maple syrup, almond butter, vanilla, and ¼ cup of water and stir until incorporated. Add the banana mixture to the bowl with the dry ingredients and stir just until well combined.

4. Pour the batter into the prepared pan. Bake for 55 minutes, or until a toothpick comes out clean. Cool completely in the pan before turning the loaf out. Store covered at room temperature for 2 to 3 days.

chocolatey orange scones

MAKES 8 SCONES

We were lured by our love of dark chocolate into switching up the popular lavender blueberry scone we sold in our shop with a chocolatey orange combo, which is now even more beloved by customers. Using the same base as before, which has a crisp exterior and a soft, slightly crumbly interior, we added a hint of citrus and intense chocolate flavor. If you're feeling indulgent, add a dollop of Coconut Whipped Cream (page 44) and enjoy with afternoon tea or coffee.

1¼ cups plus 3 tablespoons oat flour

½ cup coconut palm sugar

¼ cup raw cacao powder

1 tablespoon flaxseed meal

1 tablespoon baking powder

½ teaspoon sea salt

¼ cup unrefined virgin coconut oil, melted

¼ cup full-fat coconut milk, can shaken or stirred well to recombine

Zest (about 1 teaspoon) and juice (about 2 tablespoons) from ½ medium orange

1 teaspoon pure vanilla extract or powder

½ cup raw chocolate chips or chopped raw chocolate

1. Position a rack in the center of the oven and preheat to 400°F. Line a rimmed baking sheet with parchment paper and set aside.

2. In a large bowl, whisk together the flour, sugar, cacao powder, flaxseed meal, baking powder, and salt. Add the coconut oil and stir until the mixture is crumbly and resembles sand (use your hands to combine if needed).

3. In a separate bowl, stir together the coconut milk, zest, juice, and vanilla. Add the wet ingredients to the dry ingredients and stir until just combined and the dough comes together. Fold in the chocolate.

4. Turn the dough out onto the prepared baking sheet. Using your hands, shape it into a 6-inch-wide, 1-inch-thick disk. Using a knife, divide the disk into 8 wedges and use a spatula to separate them on the baking sheet, placing them about 2 inches apart.

5. Bake for 13 minutes, or until the tops of the scones just spring back when gently pressed with your finger. Cool completely on the pan before serving.

chocolate-glazed doughnut holes

MAKES 22 DOUGHNUT HOLES

Just like traditional doughnut holes, these bite-size poppers are cakey and moist, and they have the added bonus of a fudgy glaze. They offer the perfect amount of sweetness in the morning without the sin of processed flours, sugars, and oils. There are only good ingredients here, including coconut, almond, flax, and cacao.

FOR THE DOUGHNUTS:

⅓ cup unrefined virgin coconut oil

2 ounces 72% or darker raw chocolate or Traditional Raw Chocolate Bar (page 34), chopped

4 Flax Eggs (page 47)

1 cup almond flour

½ cup coconut palm sugar

6 tablespoons coconut flour

½ teaspoon baking soda

½ teaspoon sea salt

FOR THE GLAZE:

1 cup coconut palm sugar

¼ cup raw cacao powder

3 tablespoons full-fat coconut milk, can shaken or stirred well to recombine

1 teaspoon pure vanilla powder

1. Position a rack in the center of the oven and preheat to 350°F. Line a rimmed baking sheet with parchment paper and set aside.

2. **Make the doughnuts:** In a small saucepan over medium heat, combine the coconut oil and chocolate, stirring constantly until melted. Remove from the heat and whisk in the flax eggs until fully incorporated. Set aside.

3. In a large bowl, whisk together the almond flour, sugar, coconut flour, baking soda, and salt. Add the melted chocolate mixture and stir well to combine until you get a thick dough.

4. Scoop out 2 tablespoons of dough and shape into a ball, repeating until you have used all the dough. Place the dough balls at least 1 inch apart on the prepared baking sheet. Bake for 10 minutes and cool completely on the pan.

5. **While the doughnut holes cool, make the glaze:** Place the coconut sugar in a high-speed blender or food processor and run on high until a fine powder forms. Add the cacao powder and pulse

several times until combined. Pour in the coconut milk and vanilla and blend on high until smooth.

(6) Place the cooled doughnut holes on a wire rack set over parchment paper and drizzle evenly with the glaze. The doughnut holes will keep in an airtight container in the refrigerator for up to 1 week.

churro waffles
with chocolate dipping sauce

SERVES 4

Ky fell in love with churros, a sweet cinnamon pastry that's traditionally deep-fried, when she lived in Barcelona. In our healthier version, we use a waffle maker to create a crispy, browned dough that gets doused with coconut sugar and cinnamon and then cut into strips for dipping. No frying required! And the chocolate sauce, well, isn't that the reason we're all here? We think it's perfection.

FOR THE CHOCOLATE SAUCE:

¼ cup raw cacao butter, coarsely chopped, or unrefined virgin coconut oil

½ cup raw cacao powder

½ cup full-fat coconut milk, can shaken or stirred well to recombine

¼ cup pure maple syrup

FOR THE WAFFLES:

1¼ cups unrefined virgin coconut oil, melted

1 cup coconut palm sugar

3 tablespoons ground cinnamon

1 cup non-dairy milk

¼ cup almond butter

3 tablespoons pure maple syrup or coconut nectar

3 Flax Eggs (page 47)

1¼ cups cassava flour

½ teaspoon baking soda

¼ teaspoon sea salt

cassava flour

Gluten-, grain-, and nut-free, cassava flour is a great alternative to wheat flour. Made from dried cassava (also known as yuca) root—which is a tuber like potatoes or yams—this flour is one of our favorites for gluten-free baking because it has a fine, powdery texture, unlike the grainy quality many gluten-free flours possess. Note, though, that cassava flour is higher in carbohydrates than traditional wheat flour.

1. **Make the chocolate sauce:** Melt the cacao butter in a medium saucepan over low heat. Whisk in the cacao powder, coconut milk, and maple syrup until well combined. Set aside to cool slightly and thicken.

2. **Make the waffles:** Pour 1 cup of the coconut oil into a shallow bowl big enough to dip a waffle into. Set aside.

3. In a separate shallow bowl or plate, stir together the coconut sugar and cinnamon. Set aside.

recipe continues

prep note • A crispy waffle is key here. Don't hesitate to let the batter cook longer than you would a standard waffle. You want the raised edges to turn golden (and the inside to remain slightly doughy). You can also make the waffles in advance and toast them in an oven set to 375°F for 5 to 8 minutes when you're ready to serve them.

④ In a high-speed blender or food processor, combine the remaining ¼ cup of coconut oil, milk, almond butter, maple syrup, and flax eggs. Run on high for 15 seconds, or until well combined. Using a spatula, scrape down the sides of the blender. Add the flour, baking soda, and salt and blend again until you get a smooth, thick dough.

⑤ Place the dough in the waffle iron (about 1 scant cup per 7-inch round waffle) and use a spatula or spoon to spread it to within ½ inch of the edges. Close and cook according to the manufacturer's instructions until golden and crispy. This will most likely take longer than the recommended time. Allow the waffle to cool for a second before dipping first into the coconut oil and then the cinnamon and sugar mixture, coating both sides. Repeat until all the dough is used. Cut the waffles into strips and serve immediately with the chocolate sauce for dipping.

6

raw candies and treats

We started making Almond Butter Cups (page 98) years ago and they are still one of our bestsellers in the shop. They were such a success that we were inspired to make healthier versions of all the candies and confections we enjoyed as kids. In this chapter you'll find recipes for some of our favorites, including Healthy Snickers (page 101), No-Bake Thin Mints (page 114), and Almond Joy Bars (page 108). We've developed caramel, chocolate, and even shortbread crusts that require no oven and no guilt about eating.

almond butter cups

MAKES 10 CUPS

We developed this riff on Reese's Peanut Butter Cups years ago, and now our Almond Butter Cups are one of our bestsellers. When made from high-quality, wholesome ingredients, the already-irresistible chocolate and almond butter combination becomes the tastiest rendition imaginable. Unlike the mass-market candy, which contains ingredients like TBHQ, a petroleum-derived and potentially toxic compound, our version uses only simple ingredients. But let's not talk about why you shouldn't eat the other ones—make these, and you'll see why they are the superior option!

½ cup plus 1 tablespoon unrefined virgin coconut oil

¼ cup raw cacao butter, coarsely chopped

¾ cup raw cacao powder

¼ cup pure maple syrup

½ teaspoon pure vanilla extract or powder

Pinch sea salt

⅓ cup almond butter

1. Place 10 standard-size cupcake paper liners on a rimmed baking sheet. Set aside.

2. In a small saucepan over low heat, combine the coconut oil and cacao butter, stirring occasionally until melted. Remove from the heat and whisk in the cacao powder, maple syrup, vanilla, and salt until smooth. Pour 1 tablespoon of the chocolate mixture into each cupcake liner. Place the baking sheet in the freezer for 15 minutes, or until the chocolate is firm to the touch.

3. Remove the tray from the freezer. Add a generous teaspoon of almond butter to each cup, evenly spreading it over the chocolate, and pour another tablespoon of chocolate on top to cover completely. Place the tray back in the freezer to set for another 15 minutes before serving. Store covered in the refrigerator for up to 2 weeks.

prep note • Standard paper cupcake liners placed on a baking sheet work perfectly as forms for these candies. No need to use a cupcake pan or other mold.

white chocolate
peanut butter cups,
page 100

white chocolate peanut butter cups

MAKES ABOUT 10 CUPS

Once we saw how successful our Almond Butter Cups (page 98) were, Bennett was inspired to make a white chocolate version. A combination of cacao and cashew butters make the "chocolate" extra creamy. We fill these with peanut butter, but you can use any nut butter you like, or even a dollop of the Original Chocolate Spread (page 42) in the center to appease dark chocolate lovers. Any way you fill 'em, these cups are an excellent afternoon snack or anytime pick-me-up.

1½ cups raw cacao butter, coarsely chopped

½ cup cashew butter

1 cup pure maple syrup

½ cup raw cashews

½ teaspoon pure vanilla extract or powder

Pinch sea salt

⅔ cup peanut butter

1. Place 10 standard-size cupcake paper liners on a rimmed baking sheet. Set aside.

2. In a small saucepan over low heat, combine the cacao and cashew butters, stirring occasionally until melted. Pour the melted butters into a high-speed blender or food processor and add the maple syrup, cashews, vanilla, and salt and puree, scraping down the sides as needed, until smooth and no nut pieces remain.

3. Pour 1 generous tablespoon of the mixture into each cupcake liner. Place the baking sheet in the freezer for 15 minutes, or until the white chocolate is firm to the touch.

4. Remove the baking sheet from the freezer. Add a tablespoon of peanut butter to each cup, spreading it evenly over the bottom layer, and pour another generous tablespoon of white chocolate on top to cover completely. Place the baking sheet back in the freezer to set for another 15 minutes. These will keep in the refrigerator for up to 2 weeks.

healthy snickers

MAKES 18 BARS

This recipe is the result of post-pregnancy hormones, a big jar of caramel sauce in the fridge, and a monstrous Snickers craving. Knowing she was craving the nutty-chocolate-nougat combination and not the candy bar itself, Ky started experimenting with the leftover caramel and cashews as a replacement for peanuts because of their extra-creamy texture. Making three layers may seem like a daunting task, but it's not—waiting for the layers to set is the hardest part. After you've made these bars once, you'll want them to be ready to eat NOW.

FOR THE CHOCOLATE BASE:

¼ **cup raw cacao butter, coarsely chopped**

¼ **cup coconut butter**

½ **cup raw cacao powder**

¼ **cup pure maple syrup**

FOR THE NOUGAT:

¾ **cup cashew butter**

½ **cup coconut butter**

1 **teaspoon unrefined virgin coconut oil**

3 **tablespoons raw honey or pure maple syrup**

½ **teaspoon pure vanilla powder**

1. Line a 9 x 5-inch pan with parchment paper, leaving an overhang on two opposite sides. Set aside.

2. **Make the chocolate base:** In a small saucepan over low heat, combine the cacao and coconut butters and cook until melted. Add the cacao powder and maple syrup and whisk until completely smooth and no clumps remain. Pour the chocolate mixture into the prepared pan. Place in the freezer until set, about 30 minutes.

3. **While the chocolate firms, make the nougat layer:** In a small saucepan over low heat, combine the cashew and coconut butters and coconut oil, whisking constantly until completely smooth. Stir in the honey and vanilla until the mixture is incorporated to a spreadable consistency.

4. Once the chocolate has set, spread the nougat evenly over the chilled chocolate layer. Place the pan back in the freezer for 20 more minutes.

recipe and ingredients continue

FOR THE CARAMEL:

½ cup almond butter

½ cup pure maple syrup

2 tablespoons pure vanilla bean paste

1 tablespoon unrefined virgin coconut oil

¼ teaspoon sea salt

FOR THE TOPPING:

¾ cup whole raw cashews

6. **While the nougat layer chills, make the caramel:** Combine the almond butter, maple syrup, vanilla, coconut oil, and salt in a food processor and process until smooth and creamy.

7. After the nougat has fully set, remove the pan from the freezer and use a spatula to spread the caramel evenly on top. Top with the cashews. Return to the freezer for 10 more minutes, then cut into nine 1 x 5-inch bars and then cut those in half again to yield 18. Store in an airtight container in the refrigerator for up to 1 month or in the freezer for up to 3 months.

pomegranate
truffles, page 106

cookie
dough bites

be ballsy
energy balls,
page 107

cookie dough bites

MAKES 15 BITES

Who can resist a spoonful of cookie dough? Not us, that's for sure, which is why we created this egg-free version you can safely eat right out of the bowl. We shape the dough into little balls to make this treat perfect for sharing, but you don't have to. Just keep the mixture covered in the fridge and eat a spoonful as needed.

1½ cups almond flour

½ cup coconut palm sugar

⅓ cup unrefined virgin coconut oil, melted

1 teaspoon pure vanilla extract or powder

1 cup (8 ounces) coarsely chopped Traditional Raw Chocolate Bar (page 34) or chocolate chips

① Line a large plate with parchment paper and set aside.

② In a medium bowl, whisk together the flour and sugar. Stir in the coconut oil and vanilla. Sprinkle the mixture with 2 tablespoons of water and stir again until the mixture is completely moistened. Fold in the chopped chocolate.

③ Using your hands, shape the dough into tablespoon-size balls and put them on the prepared plate. Refrigerate for 30 minutes, or until the cookie dough is firm. Store in an airtight container in the refrigerator for up to 1 week.

prep note • We find some folks have very strong preferences when it comes to chips versus chunks in their cookies and, in this case, dough. When chopping your own chunks, you'll get some smaller slivers, which we suggest folding in as well. The more chocolate the better!

pomegranate truffles

MAKES 10 TRUFFLES

These truffles deliver the very essence of raw, organic cacao. We added antioxidant-rich pomegranate powder to highlight the cacao's dark, bittersweet flavor, and a touch of cinnamon, known for its mood-lifting properties. Rolling the truffles into balls can get pretty messy, but don't let this stop you. The end product is worth cocoa-covered hands.

7 ounces finely chopped (about 1½ cups) 72% or darker raw chocolate or Traditional Raw Chocolate Bar (page 34)

¾ cup full-fat coconut milk, can shaken or stirred well to recombine

1½ teaspoons pomegranate powder, or superfood fruit powder of your choice, such as acai

¼ teaspoon ground cinnamon

¼ cup raw cacao powder, for coating the truffles

① Place the chocolate in a heatproof bowl.

② In a small saucepan over medium heat, bring the coconut milk to a simmer. Remove from the heat, then pour it over the chocolate. Allow the mixture to stand for a few minutes, then stir until it's smooth and glossy. Add the pomegranate powder and cinnamon and stir to combine.

③ Place the bowl in the refrigerator for 1 to 2 hours, until it is completely firm. You can poke the middle with a knife to ensure it is firm.

④ Add the cacao powder to a small bowl and set aside.

⑤ Line a small tray or plate with wax or parchment paper. Using a small spoon, scoop up 1 tablespoon of the chocolate mixture at a time and use your hands to shape the chocolate into smooth balls. Roll the truffles in the cacao powder and coat completely.

⑥ Serve at room temperature. Store the truffles in an airtight container in the refrigerator for up to 2 weeks.

be ballsy energy balls

MAKES 16 BALLS

These energy balls are hands down one of the most popular treats in our shop. We stopped making them for a time and thought our customers were going to riot outside our doors, but we've since added them back onto our menu. Made with only four ingredients (okay, five if you use cinnamon) yet filled with protein, fiber, and healthy fats, they are ideal for a light breakfast or a quick snack. Like our customers, you, too, may become addicted. Thankfully they're extremely easy to make so you can be eating them within minutes!

1 cup shelled walnuts
1 cup pitted dates
½ cup coconut palm sugar
½ cup raw cacao powder
1 teaspoon ground cinnamon (optional)

1. Line a plate or tray with parchment paper and set aside.

2. Add the walnuts to a food processor and process until they become a powder. Add the dates and pulse several times until just combined. Add the sugar, cacao powder, and cinnamon, if using, and pulse a few more times, until it comes together and binds well.

3. Using a rubber spatula, scrape the mixture onto the parchment-lined plate. Place a heaping tablespoon of the dough into the palm of your hand and roll until smooth. Repeat with the rest of the mixture until all the dough is used. Eat immediately or store in an airtight container in the refrigerator for up to 2 weeks.

almond joy bars

MAKES 6 BARS

Chocolate and coconut are an irresistible pairing, especially for Bennett's husband, who is a huge fan of these bars. Before Bennett started making these, her husband would eat buckets of ice cream at night, but now, he instead savors one of these extremely satisfying and seemingly decadent bars, replacing refined sugars and dairy with better-for-you ingredients. It's a win-win. Bennett is happy her husband's eating healthier and he still finds joy (no pun intended) in an after-dinner treat.

FOR THE BARS:

½ cup unsweetened shredded coconut

⅓ cup coconut nectar

¼ cup finely chopped almonds

Pinch sea salt

12 whole raw almonds

FOR THE CHOCOLATE COATING:

¼ cup raw cacao butter, coarsely chopped

¼ cup coconut butter

⅓ cup raw cacao powder

⅓ cup pure maple syrup

½ teaspoon pure vanilla extract or powder

1. Line a rimmed baking sheet with parchment paper. Set aside.

2. **Make the bars:** In a medium bowl, stir together the coconut, coconut nectar, chopped almonds, and salt. Using your hands, shape the mixture into six 2½-inch-long bars and place on the prepared baking sheet. Press 2 whole almonds on top of each bar. Place the bars in the freezer to firm up, about 30 minutes.

3. **While the bars are freezing, make the chocolate coating:** In a small saucepan over medium-low heat, stir together the cacao and coconut butters until fully melted. Remove from the heat and add the cacao powder, maple syrup, and vanilla, and whisk until smooth. Allow the chocolate to cool for 15 minutes, or until it's room temperature. The chocolate will be somewhat thick.

4. Remove the bars from the freezer and spoon the chocolate over each bar to coat. Place them in the refrigerator to set for 20 minutes. Store in an airtight container in the refrigerator for up to 2 weeks.

cashew caramel clusters

MAKES 12 CLUSTERS

These dark chocolate caramel nut clusters were inspired by Bennett's dad, who used to sneak off to the candy store after dinner to buy his favorite turtles. While pecans are traditionally used, you can use any nut here. Almonds work well, and Brazil nuts would work, too. We like to use cashews because of their creamy flavor and subtle notes of sweetness, but honestly, any variety will deliver that caramel-chocolate-nut trinity. These treats are sure to get Dad's approval.

48 raw cashews (about ½ cup)

½ teaspoon unrefined virgin coconut oil, melted

FOR THE CARAMEL:

¼ cup coconut nectar

3 tablespoons almond butter

2 tablespoons unrefined virgin coconut oil, melted

½ teaspoon pure vanilla extract or powder

Pinch sea salt

FOR THE CHOCOLATE:

¼ cup raw cacao butter, coarsely chopped

¼ cup coconut butter

⅓ cup raw cacao powder

6 tablespoons pure maple syrup

½ teaspoon pure vanilla extract or powder

1. Position a rack in the center of the oven and preheat to 350°F. Line a rimmed baking sheet with parchment paper and set aside.

2. Place the cashews on the prepared baking sheet and toss with the coconut oil. Roast for 6 minutes, then set aside until cool enough to handle.

3. On the baking sheet, form the cashews into 12 x-shape clusters (4 cashews to a cluster).

4. **Make the caramel:** Combine the coconut nectar, almond butter, coconut oil, vanilla, and salt in a food processor and run until smooth. Spoon 1 generous teaspoon of caramel over each nut cluster and place in the freezer for 20 minutes.

5. **While the clusters are in the freezer, make the chocolate coating:** In a small saucepan over medium-low heat, cook the cacao and coconut butters until fully melted. Add the cacao powder, maple syrup, and vanilla and whisk until smooth.

⑥ Gently spoon 1 tablespoon of the chocolate coating over each cluster and place back in the freezer for another 30 minutes, or until the chocolate is firm to the touch. Store in an airtight container in the refrigerator for up to 2 weeks or in the freezer for up to 2 months.

samoas bars

MAKES 10 BARS

As Ky loves to do, she converted one of her favorite childhood treats into a healthier version. Using a combination of heart-healthy walnuts, protein-rich nut butter, and coconut, which contains fiber, she created a scrumptious grain-free, whole foods treat that tastes just like the beloved Samoas Girl Scout cookies she was looking to replicate. These bars may seem super indulgent, but because we make them with clean, nutritive ingredients, you can actually enjoy them guilt-free—and you'll feel satiated with just a few bites.

FOR THE CHOCOLATE BASE:

¾ cup unrefined virgin coconut oil

¾ cup raw cacao powder

3 tablespoons pure maple syrup or agave nectar

FOR THE COOKIE LAYER:

2 cups walnut flour or almond flour (page 46)

¼ cup coconut flour

1 cup unsweetened shredded coconut

¼ cup pure maple syrup or raw honey

1 teaspoon pure vanilla powder

¼ teaspoon sea salt

① Line a 9 x 5-inch pan with parchment paper, leaving an overhang on two opposite sides. Set aside.

② **Make the chocolate base:** In a small saucepan over low heat, melt the coconut oil. Remove from the heat, then whisk in the cacao powder and maple syrup until smooth. Set aside ¼ cup of the chocolate mixture. Pour the rest into the prepared pan and transfer to the freezer until firm to the touch, about 20 minutes.

③ **While the chocolate is in the freezer, make the cookie layer:** Combine the flours, coconut, maple syrup, vanilla, and salt in a food processor and run for 90 seconds, or until a loose dough forms and it sticks together when you press the mixture between your fingers (it should be smooth and sticky like cookie dough, but it will not form a ball). Gently turn the mixture out onto the chilled chocolate base. Using your fingers or an offset spatula, press the dough into an even layer over the chocolate. Place the pan back into the freezer to firm, about 15 minutes.

FOR THE CARAMEL:

¾ cup pure maple syrup

½ cup almond butter

1 tablespoon coconut butter

2 teaspoons pure vanilla powder

¼ teaspoon sea salt

FOR THE TOPPING:

1½ cups unsweetened
shredded coconut, toasted
(see Prep Note)

④ **Make the caramel:** Combine the maple syrup, almond and coconut butters, vanilla, and salt in a food processor and run until smooth and creamy. Using the back of a spoon, spread the caramel on the cookie layer.

⑤ Top with the toasted coconut. Return the pan to the freezer for at least 30 minutes, until the caramel is set.

⑥ Remove the dish from the freezer and cut into 1¾ x 2½-inch bars (you should have about 10). Drizzle with the reserved chocolate mixture. If the chocolate has hardened, heat it on low, stirring constantly until it is pourable. Store in an airtight container in the refrigerator for up to 2 weeks.

prep note • No Samoas would be complete without toasted coconut, which is also a terrific topping for a plethora of foods, both sweet and savory. To toast coconut, preheat the oven to 325°F and spread the shredded coconut in a thin layer on a rimmed baking sheet lined with parchment paper. Bake for 6 minutes, stirring once halfway through. The coconut should be golden brown, and if not, let it toast another minute or two, checking every 45 seconds, as it tends to burn quickly. Set aside to cool completely before using.

no-bake thin mints

MAKES ABOUT 14 COOKIES

Another Girl Scout cookie we adored growing up was the Thin Mint, but now we know they contain high fructose corn syrup and artificial flavors. In our version, we eliminate those unwanted ingredients and use oat flour, which can help stabilize blood sugar levels. When you bite into a chilled cookie, it's like a cool, chocolatey breeze of mint. These cookies are great for a summertime refresher, but we enjoy them year-round (think hot chocolate dippers!).

FOR THE COOKIES:

1 cup oat flour

⅓ cup raw cacao powder

¼ teaspoon sea salt

3 tablespoons unrefined virgin coconut oil, melted

3 tablespoons pure maple syrup

½ teaspoon peppermint extract

¼ teaspoon pure vanilla extract or powder, or the seeds scraped from 1 whole vanilla bean

FOR THE CHOCOLATE COATING:

⅓ cup unrefined virgin coconut oil

⅓ cup raw cacao powder

1 tablespoon pure maple syrup

⅛ teaspoon peppermint oil

1. Line a rimmed baking sheet with parchment paper and set aside.

2. **Make the cookies:** In a medium bowl, whisk together the flour, cacao powder, and salt until no clumps remain (you may have to use your fingers to break them up). Stir in the coconut oil, maple syrup, peppermint extract, and vanilla. Add 2 tablespoons of water and continue to stir until the dough forms a ball. Use your hands, if needed, to squeeze the dough together.

3. Lay a piece of parchment paper on a flat work surface. Turn the dough out onto it and, using the palm of your hands or an offset spatula, flatten it into a ⅛-inch-thick round. Cut out the cookies using a jar lid or 1¾-inch round cookie cutter. Transfer the cut cookies to the prepared baking sheet and immediately place in the freezer.

4. **While the cookies chill, make the chocolate coating:** Melt the coconut oil in a small saucepan over low heat. Remove from the heat and add the cacao powder, maple syrup, and peppermint oil, whisking until the mixture is completely smooth. Pour the chocolate mixture into a small bowl and

place it in the refrigerator to chill for 40 minutes, or until completely cool to the touch. The chocolate will thicken (it may start to harden around the edges of the bowl). It should still be runny enough to drizzle over the cookies. Before using, scrape the edges of the bowl and whisk until smooth and incorporated.

5. Remove the cookies from the freezer and pour a spoonful of the chocolate coating onto each cookie. Use the back of the spoon to evenly spread the chocolate. Repeat until all the cookies are covered. Place the cookies back in the freezer for 5 minutes to set.

6. Store the cookies in an airtight container in the refrigerator for up to 2 weeks.

salted seed and crispy rice bars

MAKES 20 BARS

These bars are like grown-up Rice Krispies Treats, but we've upgraded from marshmallows and puffed white rice cereal to more virtuous ingredients like honey, raw seeds, brown rice cereal, and tahini, or sesame seed paste, which adds richness and calcium (it has more than triple the amount per tablespoon than cow's milk). You can use any combination of nuts and seeds you like; for crunchier bars, try adding chopped almonds or macadamia nuts. You can also change up the sweeteners—agave and coconut nectar work nicely. Just keep the amounts the same and substitute away.

FOR THE BARS:

1 cup raw sunflower seeds

1 cup raw sesame seeds

3 cups puffed or crispy brown rice cereal

2 tablespoons black chia seeds

¾ cup raw honey

¾ cup pure maple syrup

½ cup tahini

1½ teaspoons sea salt

FOR THE CHOCOLATE TOPPING:

¼ cup raw cacao butter

1 tablespoon coconut butter

¼ cup raw cacao powder

2 tablespoons pure maple syrup

① Position a rack in the middle of the oven and preheat to 350°F. Line a baking sheet with parchment paper.

② Spread the sunflower and sesame seeds on the prepared pan in a single layer. Toast the seeds in the oven for 10 to 12 minutes, stirring halfway through, until fragrant and slightly golden. Set aside.

③ **Make the bars:** Line an 8 x 8-inch pan with parchment paper, leaving an overhang on two opposite sides, and set aside.

④ In a large mixing bowl, combine the brown rice puffs, toasted seeds, and chia seeds.

⑤ In a small saucepan over medium heat, cook the honey and maple syrup until the mixture just begins to bubble. Remove from the heat and whisk in the tahini and salt until smooth. If the tahini is not incorporating, return the saucepan

recipe continues

to the stove and continue to whisk over low heat until well combined. Pour the warm mixture into the bowl with the puffed rice and seeds and gently toss to coat. Using a rubber spatula, scrape the sticky mixture into the prepared dish. Using an offset spatula or the back of a spoon, firmly press into an even layer. Place the pan in the freezer for 15 minutes, or until firm.

6) **Meanwhile, make the chocolate topping:** In a small saucepan over medium-low heat, stir together the cacao and coconut butters until fully melted. Remove the pan from the heat and whisk in the cacao powder and maple syrup until smooth. Using a rubber spatula, spread the chocolate over the chilled seed-rice mixture. Place the pan in the refrigerator to chill for at least 1 hour, or until the chocolate is firm to the touch. Cut into about twenty 1¾ x 2-inch bars before serving. Store in an airtight container in the refrigerator for up to 1 week.

white chocolate fudge

MAKES 15 SQUARES

As we do with many of our recipes, we like to develop an adaptation for white chocolate fans. This luscious fudge gets its creamy, milky characteristics from a blend of cashews and cacao butter. White chocolate naturally has a subtle flavor, which creates an ideal base for other flavors; if you like, sprinkle a handful of dried or fresh fruit over the fudge and press down with an offset spatula before chilling.

1 cup raw cacao butter, coarsely chopped

½ cup pure maple syrup

Splash pure vanilla extract

Pinch sea salt

1 cup cashews

1. Line a 9 x 5-inch loaf pan with parchment paper, leaving an overhang on two opposite sides, and set aside.

2. Melt the cacao butter in a small saucepan over low heat. Remove from the heat and whisk in the maple syrup, vanilla, and salt until combined. Set aside to cool for a few minutes.

3. In a food processor, pulse the cashews until they form a fine crumble. Add the butter-syrup mixture and puree until smooth. Pour the mixture into the prepared pan and place in the refrigerator to chill until firm, about 1 hour.

4. Cut the fudge into fifteen 1 x 3-inch squares and serve at room temperature. Store in an airtight container in the refrigerator for up to 2 weeks.

dark chocolate fudge

MAKES 15 SQUARES

Like in many vacation spots, fudge is a beloved summertime treat here on the island. Bennett used to eat pounds of it, never thinking twice about all the butter, refined sugar, and evaporated milk she was consuming. We've updated this old-time favorite, achieving a confection that has the same smooth, melt-in-your-mouth texture but is a whole lot better for you because of the pure ingredients.

1 cup unrefined virgin coconut oil, melted

1 cup coconut nectar

1 cup raw cacao powder

Splash pure vanilla extract

Pinch sea salt

1. Line a 9 x 5-inch loaf pan with parchment paper, leaving an overhang on two opposite sides, and set aside.

2. Combine the coconut oil, coconut nectar, cacao powder, vanilla, and salt in a high-speed blender and puree until smooth. Pour the mixture into the prepared pan and place in the refrigerator to chill until firm, about 1 hour.

3. Cut the fudge into fifteen 1 x 3-inch squares and serve at room temperature. Store in an airtight container in the refrigerator for up to 2 weeks.

prep note • You can use any size pan, depending on how thick you like your fudge.

white chocolate fudge,
page 119

crunchy rice bark with sea salt

MAKES ABOUT 15 PIECES

Ky's family loves Nestlé Crunch, those milk chocolate bars with crisped rice. She created this version for her brother Drew, who wanted a crunchy bar with a sprinkle of sea salt. Ky ramped up the cacao content, so while these are darker than the original Nestlé bars, they still have that recognizable and delicious crispy crunch.

¾ cup crispy or puffed rice cereal

1 cup plus 1 teaspoon raw cacao butter, coarsely chopped

1 cup raw cacao powder

½ cup pure maple syrup

½ teaspoon flaky sea salt

prep note • You have the option of using crispy or puffed rice cereal here, with the crispy variety creating a more distinctive "crunch." For an alternative treat, you can make small crunch cups by dividing the cereal among liners and then pouring the chocolate over it.

① Line a rimmed baking sheet with parchment paper. Sprinkle the cereal over the prepared baking sheet to form a 10-inch square and set aside.

② In a small saucepan over low heat, melt the cacao butter. Remove from the heat and whisk in the cacao powder and maple syrup until combined and smooth. Immediately pour the chocolate over the cereal, scraping it from the pan with a rubber spatula and gently spreading it into a rough 12-inch square. The mixture will be thick and the cereal may spread; if it does, just scatter it back on top of the chocolate. Sprinkle the salt on top.

③ Chill in the freezer for 1 hour, or until the chocolate is firm to the touch. Remove the baking sheet from the freezer and gently break the chocolate into 2- to 3-inch pieces. Store in an airtight container in the refrigerator for up to 1 week.

chocolate bark
with fresh pomegranate seeds

MAKES ABOUT 15 PIECES

Our very first holiday bar was called Be Jolly and although we no longer sell it, it's still one of our favorites. We've made an update though, replacing the pomegranate powder used in our beloved special edition with fresh pomegranate. With each bite, the seeds, crunchy and juicy, burst in your mouth. The ruby-red jewels are more than just pretty, though; they are rich in antioxidants and micronutrients, so you're getting a double dose by pairing them with cacao. We like to serve this bark after a holiday meal, but of course it's delicious any time of year.

Seeds of ½ pomegranate
  (about ½ cup)

1 cup plus 1 teaspoon raw cacao
  butter, coarsely chopped

1 cup raw cacao powder

½ cup pure maple syrup

prep note • To quickly remove the pomegranate seeds, roll the fruit on the counter to loosen the seeds, then use a sharp knife to score around the middle of the fruit and break it apart. Holding each half over a bowl, seed-side facing down, tap the outside with a wooden spoon, squeezing a little to release the seeds.

1. Line a rimmed baking sheet with parchment paper. Scatter the pomegranate seeds generously over the prepared sheet to form a 12-inch square. Set aside.

2. In a small saucepan over low heat, melt the cacao butter. Remove from the heat and whisk in the cacao powder and maple syrup until smooth and fully combined.

3. Immediately pour the chocolate over the seeds, using a rubber spatula to scrape it out of the pan and spread it evenly into a rough 12-inch square. Chill in the refrigerator until the chocolate is firm to the touch, about 1 hour. Remove the baking sheet from the refrigerator and gently break the chocolate into 2- to 3-inch pieces.

4. Store in an airtight container in the refrigerator for 3 to 5 days, depending on the freshness of the pomegranate.

mocha chocolate bark

MAKES ABOUT 15 PIECES

Peanut butter and jelly. Strawberries and cream. Coffee and chocolate. Some foods just taste better when they're together, and this bark is the perfect example. A sprinkling of coffee on the chocolate gives it an extra kick and a lovely, bitter contrast to the sweet, sublime chocolate. If chocolate and coffee are your vices, this bar is for you!

1 cup raw cacao powder

¾ cup unrefined virgin coconut oil, melted

⅓ cup pure maple syrup

½ teaspoon sea salt

1 tablespoon ground coffee

① Line a rimmed baking sheet with parchment paper. Set aside.

② In a medium bowl, whisk together the cacao powder, coconut oil, maple syrup, and salt until smooth. Pour the chocolate onto the prepared baking sheet and, using a rubber spatula, scrape down the sides of the bowl and spread the chocolate into a rough 12-inch square. Sprinkle the chocolate with the coffee. Chill in the refrigerator until the chocolate is firm to the touch, about 30 minutes. Remove the baking sheet from the refrigerator and gently break the chocolate into 2- to 3-inch pieces.

③ Store in an airtight container in the refrigerator for up to 1 week.

prep note • If your kitchen is warm, this bark will become very soft and may melt if it's kept out of the refrigerator. Be sure to keep this bark in a cool place before serving, or eat straight from the fridge.

raw desserts

This sweet chapter is filled with special
occasion desserts like trifles and pot de crème.
Individual servings of a rich chocolate pudding
always make an elegant ending to a celebratory meal,
as does the presentation of a cloudlike cream pie.
These from-scratch desserts will impress your
guests not only because they're pretty but also
because the wholesome ingredients will leave
them feeling happy and satiated.

apple nachos

SERVES 4

These are nacho normal nachos. No tortilla chips or cheese here. Our version uses apples and, of course, chocolate. We like to drizzle on caramel, too, but the list of toppings you can add after that is endless. Get creative and use your favorite pairings—pecans and coconut, mango and macadamia, almonds and cherries. When we say this recipe is easy, we really mean it. And it looks so pretty, which makes it a fabulous option for a party.

FOR THE CHOCOLATE SAUCE:

¼ cup pure maple syrup

¼ cup raw cacao powder

FOR THE CARAMEL SAUCE:

¼ cup coconut nectar

3 tablespoons almond butter

2 tablespoons unrefined virgin coconut oil, melted

½ teaspoon pure vanilla extract or powder

Pinch sea salt

TO ASSEMBLE:

3 apples, any variety, cored and thinly sliced

Chopped nuts, dried fruit, or toasted shredded coconut, for serving (optional)

1. **Make the chocolate sauce:** In a small saucepan over medium-low heat, whisk together the maple syrup and cacao powder until smooth. Set aside.

2. **Make the caramel sauce:** Add the coconut nectar, almond butter, coconut oil, vanilla, and salt to a food processor and puree until completely smooth. Set aside.

3. **Assemble the nachos:** Spread the apple slices onto a platter or serving tray in a single even layer. Pour the chocolate and caramel sauces over the apples and sprinkle with the toppings of your choice. Serve immediately.

pumpkin cheesecake bites

MAKES ABOUT 28 BITES

Inspired by *Green Kitchen Stories*, one of our favorite vegetarian blogs, this recipe delivers all the warm flavors we crave in fall: pumpkin, cinnamon, ginger, and nutmeg. We've tweaked their recipe to make it our own by dipping the divine little squares of pumpkin cheesecake into a homemade chocolate coating. These little bites may be eaten frozen and, since they can be prepared completely in advance, are a great addition to any holiday meal.

FOR THE COCONUT CRUST:

¾ cup pitted dates, soaked in hot water for **10 minutes**, then drained, plus more as needed

1 tablespoon unrefined virgin coconut oil

1 cup unsweetened shredded coconut

FOR THE PUMPKIN FILLING:

One 15-ounce can pumpkin puree (about 2 cups)

½ cup tightly packed pitted dates, soaked in hot water for **10 minutes**, then drained

¼ cup cashew butter

2 tablespoons unrefined virgin coconut oil

1 teaspoon ground cinnamon

½ teaspoon ground ginger

¼ teaspoon freshly ground nutmeg

¼ teaspoon pure vanilla extract or powder

¼ teaspoon sea salt

① Line an 8 x 8-inch square pan with parchment paper, leaving an overhang on two opposite sides. Set aside.

② **Make the crust:** In the bowl of a food processor, combine the soaked dates with the coconut oil and shredded coconut. Puree until a dough forms, scraping down the sides of the bowl with a spatula as necessary. If it is too dry, add a few more soaked dates and puree again. Transfer the mixture to the prepared pan and, using an offset spatula or the back of a spoon, firmly press the mixture into an even layer.

③ **Make the pumpkin filling:** In a food processor, combine the pumpkin, dates, cashew butter, coconut oil, cinnamon, ginger, nutmeg, vanilla, and salt and puree until smooth. Pour the pumpkin filling over the coconut crust and place in the freezer until firm and your finger barely makes an indent, about 2 hours.

recipe and ingredients continue

FOR THE CHOCOLATE COATING:

½ cup unrefined virgin coconut oil

1 heaping tablespoon coconut butter

½ cup raw cacao powder

2 tablespoons pure maple syrup

prep note • You may use 1½ teaspoons of pumpkin pie spice as a substitution for the cinnamon, ginger, nutmeg, and vanilla. Be sure the pumpkin cheesecake is completely frozen before you cut it into squares and dip it in the chocolate. Alternately, you can pour a layer of chocolate on top of the frozen pumpkin layer, let it set in the freezer, then cut the cheesecake into bite-size pieces.

④ **Make the chocolate coating:** In a small saucepan over medium-low heat, heat the coconut oil and butter until fully melted. Add the cacao powder and maple syrup and whisk until smooth. Remove from the heat and allow to cool to room temperature.

⑤ Set a wire rack over a baking sheet lined with parchment paper. Remove the cheesecake from the freezer and, pulling the sides of parchment, gently lift it from the pan. If it doesn't come out easily, run a knife along the edges. Cut the cheesecake into 1¼-inch squares and transfer them to the rack.

⑥ Using a fork, gently lower a cheesecake square into the chocolate to completely coat, then return it to the wire rack. Repeat with each square. Place the wire rack with the cheesecake bites set over the baking sheet in the freezer until the bites firm slightly, about 30 minutes. Store the squares in an airtight container in the refrigerator, where they will remain soft and cheesecakelike for up to 4 days.

truffle pudding

SERVES 4 TO 6

This luscious truffle pudding begins with a gooey chocolate walnut base layer and is topped off with two layers of velvety chocolate cream. We combine almond milk with cashew butter and coconut oil to keep the texture light and fluffy but firm enough to stand up to all the rich chocolate flavor. These individual desserts can be assembled in all different three-quarter-cup containers depending on the occasion; you can fancy them up by serving them in antique custard cups with silver spoons or dress them down in mini Ball jars.

FOR THE CHOCOLATE WALNUT BASE:

½ cup shelled walnuts

½ cup pitted dates

2 tablespoons raw cacao powder

FOR THE DARK TRUFFLE LAYER:

¾ cup almond milk

½ cup unrefined virgin coconut oil

½ cup cashew butter

¼ cup pure maple syrup

2 tablespoons raw cacao powder

2 teaspoons pure vanilla powder

¼ teaspoon sea salt

FOR THE LIGHT TRUFFLE LAYER:

½ cup almond milk

1. **Make the chocolate walnut base:** In a food processor, pulse the walnuts until fine. Add the dates and cacao powder and process until a sticky dough forms. Divide the mixture among six 6-ounce ramekins or containers, about 2 tablespoons each, and using slightly damp fingers, press an even ¼-inch base into the bottom of each dish.

2. **Make the dark truffle layer:** In a high-speed blender, combine the almond milk, coconut oil, cashew butter, maple syrup, cacao powder, vanilla, and salt and puree until creamy and thick, about 30 seconds. Fill each ramekin about two-thirds full (you'll have about ¾ cup of the mixture left in the blender). Place the ramekins in the refrigerator and chill until the pudding is set to the touch, about 15 minutes.

3. **Make the light truffle layer:** Add the almond milk to the dark truffle mixture remaining in the blender and puree until smooth. When the dark truffle layer is set, pour the light truffle mixture over each ramekin. Chill for another 45 minutes before serving. Store, covered, in the refrigerator for up to 1 week.

pot de crème

SERVES 6

Bennett has never been a fan of classic French desserts; however, her aunt makes a lush, rich pot de crème she just can't resist. In an effort to healthify her aunt's recipe, Bennett replaced each ingredient, including eggs, cream, and white sugar, with plant-based, whole foods options like almond milk, almond butter, a small amount of coconut sugar, and good raw chocolate. The result is still a decadently smooth custard but without refined ingredients. This dessert can be put together in minutes, though it needs to chill for two hours before serving, so make sure you give yourself enough time. We like to spoon on a dollop of Coconut Whipped Cream (page 44), which adds a light creaminess to the mousse by cutting the bitterness of the chocolate. If you're sharing this with guests, they are guaranteed to swoon.

1½ cups almond milk

¼ cup coconut nectar

¼ cup almond butter

2 tablespoons coconut palm sugar

½ teaspoon pure vanilla extract or powder

9 ounces 72% or darker raw dark chocolate or Traditional Raw Chocolate Bar (page 34), chopped

Coconut Whipped Cream, for serving (page 44)

① In a small saucepan over medium heat, combine the almond milk, coconut nectar, almond butter, sugar, and vanilla and whisk until smooth. Bring the mixture to a boil, then immediately remove from the heat.

② Add the chopped chocolate to a high-speed blender. Pour in the warm milk mixture and puree until smooth, about 30 seconds. Divide the mixture among six 4-ounce ramekins, scraping the sides of the blender jar with a rubber spatula, and chill in the refrigerator for at least 2 hours, or until the custard is set. To serve, top each ramekin with a dollop of coconut whipped cream. Store in the refrigerator, covered, for up to 2 days.

brownie trifle
with caramelized bananas

SERVES 4

Bringing this trifle to the table always guarantees *oohs* and *aahs* from guests. Perhaps it's the beautiful layers of fudgy dark chocolate brownie, caramelized bananas, and Coconut Whipped Cream (page 44) showing through the sides of the trifle bowl, or the anticipation of digging a spoon deep into that dish of deliciousness. We like serving this at intimate gatherings where none of us mind dipping into the same bowl, but of course, the trifle can be spooned out into individual servings too. If you don't have a trifle bowl, a large glass bowl works just as well.

FOR THE BROWNIE:

**2 cups pitted dates, soaked
in hot water for 10 minutes
then drained**

2 cups shelled walnuts

¾ cup raw cacao powder

¼ teaspoon ground cinnamon

Pinch sea salt

FOR THE CARAMELIZED BANANAS:

**2 tablespoons raw honey
or coconut palm sugar**

**1 tablespoon unrefined virgin
coconut oil**

**4 bananas, peeled and sliced
½ inch thick**

FOR THE TOPPING:

**About 3 cups Coconut Whipped
Cream (page 44)**

**Be Saucy Chocolate Sauce
(page 38), Coconut Caramel
Sauce (page 41), raw honey,
pure maple syrup, shaved
coconut, or raw cacao nibs, for
serving (optional)**

① **Make the brownie:** In the bowl of a food processor, combine the soaked dates, walnuts, cacao powder, cinnamon, and salt and run until a wet, sticky dough forms, scraping down the sides as needed. Some small pieces of walnut will remain. Transfer the brownie mixture to a 6-cup trifle bowl or dish and press evenly into the bottom and slightly up the sides of the dish.

② **Caramelize the bananas:** In a large nonstick pan over medium-high heat, cook the honey and coconut oil until hot, about a minute or two. Fry the banana slices in a single layer for 3 to 4 minutes, until slightly golden. Flip and fry for 1 to 2 minutes more (don't fry them for too long, otherwise the bananas will get mushy and lose their shape). Remove to a plate. Repeat until all the bananas are fried. Cool slightly, then arrange them on top of the brownie layer.

③ Spread the coconut whipped cream on top of the bananas. Drizzle with the sauces and sprinkle with the toppings of your choice. The trifle can be stored in the refrigerator, covered, for up to 1 week.

salted caramel double chocolate pie

MAKES ONE 9-INCH PIE

Making a raw pie is hands down simpler than baking one, because as the pie chills, you can chill, too. Packed with flavor, this dessert has a walnut-date crust topped with a creamy mousse-like middle layer made with avocados. This green fruit, usually reserved for guacamole, is one of our favorite dairy replacements because it lends a creamy texture without significant taste (you can always keep this avocado thing our little secret if you think it'll weird people out). The pièce de résistance: a top layer of caramel sweetened with honey and a sprinkling of sea salt.

FOR THE CRUST:

1¼ cups shelled walnuts

½ cup pitted dates

¼ cup raw cacao powder

3 tablespoons unrefined virgin coconut oil, melted

1 teaspoon pure vanilla extract or powder

Pinch salt

FOR THE FILLING:

2 ripe avocados, pitted, peeled, and cut into large chunks

⅓ cup almond butter

6 tablespoons pure maple syrup

¼ cup raw cacao powder

1 teaspoon pure vanilla extract or powder

① **Make the crust:** In the bowl of a food processor, pulse the walnuts, dates, cacao powder, coconut oil, vanilla, and salt until well combined. With damp fingers, press the mixture evenly into a 9-inch pie pan. Place the crust in the refrigerator to chill for at least 10 minutes.

② **Make the filling:** In a high-speed blender, combine the avocados, almond butter, maple syrup, cacao powder, and vanilla with 1 cup of water and puree until smooth. Pour into the chilled crust and spread in an even layer. Chill the pie in the refrigerator for 20 minutes, or until set.

FOR THE CARAMEL:

¼ cup raw honey

3 tablespoons almond butter

2 tablespoons unrefined virgin coconut oil, melted

1 teaspoon pure vanilla extract or powder

Pinch sea salt

③ **Make the caramel:** In a medium bowl, whisk together the honey, almond butter, coconut oil, vanilla, and salt until smooth. (You can also make this in a food processor.) Spread the caramel mixture on top of the chilled pie. Serve immediately or store in the refrigerator, covered, for up to 2 days.

tart coconut lime pie

MAKES ONE 9-INCH PIE

Light and fresh, this tangy pie is the perfect finish to a heavy meal. Like the Salted Caramel Double Chocolate Pie (page 140), you can whip this up in minutes. If you're really in a rush (say, if guests are arriving at your door in ten minutes), you can pop this pie in the freezer and it'll be ready to serve in less than thirty. The texture will be slightly firmer than if you refrigerated it, but it'll still be magnificently delicious.

FOR THE CRUST:

1½ cups almond flour

½ cup coconut palm sugar

¼ teaspoon sea salt

1 tablespoon unrefined virgin coconut oil, melted

1 teaspoon pure vanilla extract

1 tablespoon almond milk or water, plus more as needed

FOR THE FILLING:

1 cup solid unrefined virgin coconut oil (see Prep Note)

¼ cup pure maple syrup

1 cup coconut butter

Juice of 4 limes (about ½ cup)

¼ teaspoon pure vanilla extract or powder

½ cup raw cacao nibs, for serving

prep note • If it's warm in your kitchen and your coconut oil isn't completely solid, measure out 1 cup about 30 minutes before using and put it in the freezer to firm a bit. Be sure to measure out the oil *before* you chill it, because it can be difficult to spoon hardened oil out of a container.

1. **Make the crust:** In a large bowl, whisk together the flour, sugar, and salt. Add the coconut oil and vanilla and, using your hands, work it into the flour mixture. Add the almond milk and continue to work the mixture until it's evenly moist and doughlike. If it feels too dry, add 1 teaspoon of milk at a time until a dough forms. Bring the dough together to form a ball.

2. Transfer the dough to a 9-inch pie pan and with damp fingers press it evenly into the bottom and up the sides of the dish. Place the crust in the freezer to chill for at least 5 minutes.

3. **Make the pie filling:** Add the coconut oil and maple syrup to a high-speed blender and puree until just smooth. Add the coconut butter, lime juice, and vanilla and puree again just until smooth. Be careful not to overprocess otherwise the fats will separate. Pour the mixture over the chilled crust and place in the refrigerator for 3 to 4 hours or the freezer for 30 minutes.

4. Sprinkle with cacao nibs before serving. The pie can be stored in the refrigerator, covered, for up to 1 week.

8

baked goods

Our beginnings are rooted in raw cacao treats, but we have a major sweet spot for baked goods. We've reworked some standards, like brownies and cakes, to incorporate raw cacao and other surprising ingredients such as black beans or beets, which keep everything gluten-free and add fiber and other nutrients without sacrificing flavor. In this chapter, you'll also find Tiramisu (page 183) and our popular Chocolate Tart with Mashed Raspberries and Pine Nut Crust (page 186), which has an especially tasty pine nut shortbread crust as well as family favorites like Indoor S'mores (page 167) and crunchy Chocolate Caramel Popcorn (page 178).

chocolate birthday cake

MAKES TWO 5-INCH CAKES

Inspired by one of our favorite cakes from L.A.'s Sweet Laurel Bakery, this sweet and petite beauty is the perfect celebration cake. We use nut butter to create a frosting that is so indulgent you'll never make a traditional chocolate frosting again. The cake itself is extremely moist—it has such a dense, almost creamy texture—you may think it's underbaked, but it's not. It's small in size, but because it's sumptuous, you'll need only a little sliver to be satisfied. We've served it many times with rave reviews and hope you do, too!

FOR THE CAKE:

Coconut oil, for greasing the pans

2 cups finely ground blanched almond flour

5 tablespoons raw cacao powder

1 tablespoon ground flaxseed

½ teaspoon baking soda

½ teaspoon sea salt

2 Chia Eggs (page 47)

⅔ cup pure maple syrup

½ teaspoon pure vanilla bean paste or 1 tablespoon pure vanilla extract

1. **Make the cake:** Position a rack in the center of the oven and preheat to 350°F. Grease two 5-inch round cake pans with oil and line the bottoms with parchment paper. Set aside.

2. In a large bowl, whisk together the flour, cacao powder, flaxseed, baking soda, and salt. In a medium bowl, whisk the chia eggs, maple syrup, and vanilla together with ⅓ cup water until smooth and fully incorporated.

3. Pour the wet ingredients into the dry and stir well. The batter will be thick. Divide the batter between the two prepared pans, filling them each halfway, and bake for 25 minutes, or until a toothpick comes out clean. The cakes will look dry on top, but don't worry—they're not overbaked. Let the cakes cool in the pans, about 40 minutes, then run a small paring knife around the edges of the pan and turn them out onto a rack, removing the parchment paper, to cool completely.

recipe and ingredients continue

FOR THE CHOCOLATE FROSTING:

½ scant cup raw cacao butter, coarsely chopped

¼ cup unrefined virgin coconut oil

⅓ cup plus 2 tablespoons raw cacao powder

5 tablespoons pure maple syrup

½ teaspoon pure vanilla powder (optional)

½ cup creamy almond butter

Sliced fruit, shredded coconut, or edible flowers, for garnish (optional)

④ **Make the frosting:** In a small saucepan over low heat, cook the cacao butter and coconut oil until melted, stirring occasionally, then remove from the heat. Whisk in the cacao powder, maple syrup, and vanilla, if using, until smooth and fully combined. Add the almond butter and continue to whisk until the mixture becomes thick, like a ganache. Allow the frosting to cool to room temperature before using, about 30 minutes. Whisk again vigorously before using.

⑤ Frost the top of each cake and stack if desired. Decorate with sliced fruit, shredded coconut, or edible flowers if desired.

prep note • For a larger party, double the recipe and bake the cakes in two 9-inch cake pans to stack. For a variation on the frosting, substitute 4 ounces chopped raw chocolate for the cacao butter and powder and add 2 additional tablespoons each coconut oil and almond butter. The flavor will be slightly nuttier and less rich.

chocolate beet lava cakes

MAKES 4 CAKES

If intense chocolate flavor is your jam, then these little cakes are for you. The crumb is extremely velvety, which is a result of adding beets, a secret ingredient in our cacao kitchen arsenal. You won't taste them, but they quietly add to the nutritional value and enhance the dark chocolate flavor. For more decadence, each upside-down cupcake is topped with warm chocolate sauce. The individual serving size makes them fun for a dinner party.

FOR THE BEET CAKES:

2 medium red beets (about ¾ pound), peeled and cut into 1½-inch chunks

2 tablespoons unrefined virgin coconut oil, melted, plus more for greasing the pan

¼ cup almond milk

½ teaspoon apple cider vinegar

¾ teaspoon baking soda

3 tablespoons pure maple syrup

2 tablespoons plus 2 teaspoons coconut palm sugar

1 Flax Egg (page 47)

Pinch sea salt

½ cup almond meal

5 tablespoons raw cacao powder

3 tablespoons coconut flour

FOR THE MOLTEN LAVA SAUCE:

½ cup pure maple syrup

½ cup raw cacao powder

Coconut Whipped Cream, for serving (page 44)

① **Make the beet cakes:** Add the beets to a small saucepan, cover with water, and set over high heat. Bring to a boil, reduce the heat, and simmer for 15 minutes, or until you can pierce the beets easily with a fork. Drain them, transfer to a high-speed blender, and puree until smooth. Measure out ½ cup of the puree for the cakes. If you have any left over, save it for a smoothie.

② Position a rack in the center of the oven and preheat to 375°F. Grease 4 standard muffin cups with coconut oil. Set aside.

③ In a medium bowl, stir together the almond milk and vinegar and set aside to curdle, about 5 minutes.

④ Add the baking soda. The mixture will fizz. Stir in the ½ cup of beet puree, the maple syrup, sugar, flax egg, coconut oil, and salt and mix until well combined. Add the almond meal, cacao powder, and coconut flour and stir to combine until thick.

recipe continues

Divide the batter among the muffin cups and bake for 15 minutes, or until the tops are puffy and a toothpick inserted into a cake comes out clean.

5. Let the cakes rest in the pan for 10 to 15 minutes, then gently remove them by turning the pan over onto a cooling rack. Allow them to cool completely.

6. **Make the lava sauce:** In a small saucepan over medium heat, heat the maple syrup until it just begins to simmer. Immediately remove from the heat and whisk in the cacao powder until smooth.

7. To serve, place each cake on its own plate. Using a small spoon, make a small indentation in the top of each cake. Spoon 2 to 3 tablespoons of the molten lava sauce into each indentation so it pools on the top. Serve immediately with a dollop of coconut whipped cream.

pbh chocolate cupcakes

MAKES 10 CUPCAKES

Gluten-free cakes often have an unappealing, dry, crumbly texture, but not these babies. The crumb is perfectly moist and there are no weird additives needed to achieve it, just our usual cast of characters, including coconut milk, coconut sugar, and coconut oil. We add applesauce, as well, to create a toothsome bite. And while the texture is fantastic, it's the frosting that makes these little gems special. The combination of peanut butter and honey, what we deem PBH, makes it so sweet and creamy, you'll want to eat it by the spoonful. The downside is that the frosting melts if it's in a room that's the least bit warm; it's imperative you keep the cupcakes refrigerated until you serve them. Feel free to substitute your favorite nut butter.

FOR THE CUPCAKES:

1½ cups oat flour

1 cup coconut palm sugar

½ cup raw cacao powder

½ teaspoon baking soda

Pinch sea salt

1 cup full-fat coconut milk, can shaken or stirred well to recombine

½ cup unsweetened applesauce

¼ cup unrefined virgin coconut oil, melted

1 teaspoon apple cider vinegar

1 teaspoon pure vanilla extract or powder

1. Position a rack in the center of the oven and preheat to 350°F. Line a standard 12-cup muffin pan with 10 cupcake liners.

2. **Make the cupcakes:** In a large bowl, whisk together the flour, sugar, cacao powder, baking soda, and salt. In another bowl, stir together the coconut milk, applesauce, coconut oil, vinegar, and vanilla. Gently fold the wet ingredients into the dry until just incorporated. Divide the batter among the cupcake liners, filling them about three-quarters full. Bake for 15 minutes, or until a toothpick inserted into a cupcake comes out clean. Let the cupcakes cool completely in the pan before frosting.

FOR THE FROSTING:

½ cup peanut butter or
nut butter of your choice

½ cup solid unrefined virgin
coconut oil

¼ cup raw honey

Splash pure vanilla extract

Pinch sea salt

③ **Make the frosting:** In a medium bowl, combine the peanut butter, coconut oil, honey, vanilla, and salt and beat on medium-high with an electric hand mixer until light and fluffy. Chill the frosting for 45 minutes to stiffen. When ready to frost, whip the frosting again by hand, then frost as desired. Serve immediately or store the cupcakes in an airtight container in the refrigerator for up to 3 days.

fudgy you'll-never-again-want-to-make-box brownies

MAKES 9 BROWNIES

Brownies typically get classified as either cakey or fudgy, and these most definitely, without a doubt, fall into the latter category. They are surprisingly thin, but don't let that fool you. They have an intense cocoa flavor without being too sweet. The best part of these brownies is how the edges turn slightly chewy and crisp while the center remains soft and the teensiest bit gooey. If you like to dress up your brownies, this is a great base recipe; simply sprinkle the batter with nuts, coconut, or other toppings before baking. We'd bet good money that you'll never want to buy a boxed mix again after making these.

1 cup almond butter

⅓ cup maple syrup

2 Flax Eggs (page 47)

2 tablespoons unrefined virgin coconut oil, melted, plus more for greasing the pan

1 teaspoon pure vanilla extract

⅓ cup raw cacao powder

2 tablespoons coconut palm sugar

½ teaspoon baking soda

① Position a rack in the middle of the oven and preheat to 350°F. Grease an 8 x 8-inch baking pan with oil and line it with parchment paper, leaving an overhang on two opposite sides. Set aside.

② In a medium bowl, mix the almond butter, maple syrup, flax eggs, coconut oil, and vanilla. In a separate small bowl, whisk together the cacao powder, sugar, and baking soda until well combined, then add to the almond butter mixture.

③ Pour the batter into the prepared pan and bake for 25 minutes, or until a toothpick comes out clean. Let cool completely before cutting (the longer, the better; it will help the brownies keep their shape). Store in an airtight container at room temperature for up to 4 days.

sesame crackle cookies

MAKES 7 COOKIES

These cookies are big—in size and nutrition. In addition to oat flour, we add chickpea flour, which is rich in protein and vitamins, and one of the most nutrient-dense gluten-free flours we use. It helps build structure in baked goods and contributes to the crumb of these cookies, which is almost cakelike with a nice little fudgy chew. You may be able to detect the taste of tahini, but if not, the sesame seeds that decorate the cookies are a great clue.

¾ cup oat flour

½ cup plus 1½ tablespoons raw cacao powder

¼ cup chickpea flour

½ teaspoon baking soda

¼ teaspoon coarse sea salt

½ cup tahini

3 tablespoons unrefined virgin coconut oil

¾ cup pure maple syrup

¾ teaspoon pure vanilla extract or powder

¼ cup sesame seeds

① Position a rack in the upper and lower thirds of the oven and preheat to 325°F. Line two rimmed baking sheets with parchment paper. Set aside.

② In a large bowl, whisk together the oat flour, cacao powder, chickpea flour, baking soda, and salt.

③ In a high-speed blender or food processor, combine the tahini, coconut oil, maple syrup, and vanilla and blend until smooth and creamy. If the mixture becomes warm when processing, chill it in the refrigerator for 10 to 15 minutes to thicken it up.

④ Using a rubber spatula, scrape the tahini mixture into the dry ingredients. Stir the mixture vigorously for about 30 seconds, or until the dough comes together. Knead it with your hands for 1 to 2 minutes. Chill the dough in the refrigerator for 10 minutes.

⑤ Scoop a heaping ball of dough, about 3 tablespoons, into your hand and roll it into a ball between your

recipe continues

palms. If the dough feels too sticky to handle, return it to the refrigerator for a few minutes to firm up. Repeat to make about 7 cookies. Place the dough balls about 2 inches apart on the prepared baking sheets and sprinkle each generously with the sesame seeds.

6. Bake the cookies for 5 minutes. Remove the pans and lightly flatten each cookie using an offset spatula (the back of a standard spatula will work as well). This will create a crackle effect. Rotate the trays from front to back and top to bottom and return to the oven for 3 more minutes.

7. Let the cookies cool completely on the baking sheets before serving. Store in an airtight container at room temperature for up to 1 week.

hazelnut cranberry chocolate biscotti

MAKES 12 COOKIES

As much as we love the addictive crunch of these biscotti, our favorite part is dipping them in coffee; it's a grown-up version of milk and cookies! We've used one of our favorite flavor combinations in this recipe—chocolate and hazelnuts—and thrown in some dried cranberries for a natural source of sweetness. Dried cherries or apricots would also work here. When buying dried fruit, look for brands that are preservative-free and sweetened with apple juice instead of added sugars.

FOR THE BISCOTTI:

2 cups chopped raw hazelnuts

¼ cup pure maple syrup

3 tablespoons almond milk

2 tablespoons arrowroot powder or tapioca starch

1 tablespoon raw cacao powder

1 teaspoon pure vanilla extract or powder

½ teaspoon baking soda

¼ teaspoon sea salt

¼ cup chopped dried cranberries

FOR THE CHOCOLATE COATING:

⅓ cup raw cacao butter, coarsely chopped, or coconut butter

1 tablespoon pure maple syrup

⅓ cup raw cacao powder

① Position a rack in the center of the oven and preheat to 350°F. Line a rimmed baking sheet with parchment paper. Set aside.

② **Make the biscotti:** In a food processor, pulse 1½ cups of the hazelnuts until you have a grainy flour. Add the maple syrup, almond milk, arrowroot, cacao powder, vanilla, baking soda, and salt and pulse 4 or 5 times, until well combined. Transfer the mixture to a bowl and, using a spatula, fold in the dried cranberries and remaining ½ cup of hazelnuts.

③ Turn the dough out onto the prepared baking sheet. With slightly damp hands, shape the dough into an 11-inch-long, 2-inch-wide log (it'll be about 1 inch thick). Bake for 20 minutes, or until lightly browned and slightly cracked. It should be somewhat firm to the touch. Remove from the oven and let cool on the pan for 1 hour.

④ Preheat the oven a second time, to 250°F.

recipe continues

(5) Transfer the cooled log to a cutting board and use a sharp knife to cut it into 1-inch slices on the diagonal. Place the slices flat on a baking sheet. Bake for 10 minutes, flip, and bake for another 10 minutes. Turn off the oven and let the biscotti sit inside the oven on the baking sheet to fully cool, about 40 minutes.

(6) **Make the chocolate coating:** In a medium saucepan over low heat, melt the cacao butter, then stir in the maple syrup. Remove from the heat and whisk in the cacao powder until completely smooth. Let it cool enough, about 15 minutes, so that it sticks to the biscotti when you dip them in.

(7) Set a wire rack over a baking sheet lined with parchment paper. Dip each biscotti halfway into the sauce and transfer to the rack to let the coating set. Store the cookies in an airtight container at room temperature for up to 3 days.

chocolate-dipped coconut macaroons

MAKES ABOUT 12 MACAROONS

You can probably tell by now that we adore coconut. Not only do we believe in the fruit's many nourishing qualities, from metabolism booster to skin moisturizer, but we are huge fans of its creamy, tropical taste. These cookies deliver the very essence of that fresh coconut flavor. They come together in minutes, and the crowning glory, of course, a drizzle of chocolate. To us, these little balls of goodness are the perfect treat.

2 cups unsweetened shredded coconut

½ teaspoon sea salt

½ cup pure maple syrup

¼ cup full-fat coconut milk, can shaken or stirred well to recombine

1 teaspoon pure vanilla extract or powder

4.5 ounces 72% or darker raw chocolate, melted

1. Position a rack in the middle of the oven and preheat to 350°F. Line a rimmed baking sheet with parchment paper and set aside.

2. In a large bowl, combine the coconut and salt. Add the maple syrup, coconut milk, and vanilla and stir until well combined.

3. Using your hands, shape the mixture into golf ball–size balls and place them about an inch or so apart on the prepared baking sheet. Bake for 12 minutes, or until slightly golden. Let the macaroons cool completely on the pan. Drizzle the macaroons with the melted chocolate. Store in an airtight container at room temperature for up to 1 week.

chocolate cherry cookies

MAKES ABOUT 15 COOKIES

Any cookie that delivers protein and fiber is a hero in our book, especially if it tastes good. These cookies accomplish it all, thanks to a perhaps-unexpected ingredient: pureed black beans. In addition to contributing nutritional value, the beans make the cookies moist and chewy. We add cherries for a hint of brightness.

One 15-ounce can black beans, drained and rinsed

⅓ cup plus 2 tablespoons coconut palm sugar

6 tablespoons raw cacao powder

2 tablespoons almond flour

2 tablespoons unrefined virgin coconut oil, melted

2 teaspoons pure vanilla extract or powder

Pinch sea salt

½ cup dried tart cherries

½ cup chopped 72% or darker raw chocolate

① Position a rack in the middle of the oven and preheat to 350°F. Line a rimmed baking sheet with parchment paper and set aside.

② In the bowl of a food processor, puree the black beans until smooth, then transfer them to a medium bowl. Stir in the sugar, cacao powder, flour, coconut oil, vanilla, and salt and mix well. Fold in the cherries and raw chocolate.

③ Shape heaping tablespoons of the dough into balls and place them about an inch apart on the prepared baking sheet. Using the back of a spoon or offset spatula, slightly flatten the cookies. The dough is very sticky, so you may need to wet the spoon or spatula to press down the cookies.

④ Bake for 17 minutes, or until the cookies are slightly set (they will firm up as they cool). Let the cookies cool completely on the baking sheet. Store in an airtight container in the refrigerator for up to 3 days.

prep note • If you don't have dried cherries on hand, you can substitute dried blueberries or other dried fruit.

indoor s'mores

MAKES 4 S'MORES

This is, in our opinion, the ultimate grain-free, dairy-free version of a s'more. A crisp, light cinnamon-sugar dusted graham cracker, a thick slab of homemade chocolate, and some gooey toasted "marshmallow" cream get stacked into a messy and delicious sandwich, with no campfire required. Instead, we use a lighter or match to lightly char the marshmallow cream. When it comes to the chocolate component, our Favorite Freezer Chocolate Bar (page 35) is excellent here; because it's soft, it melts into the cracker at room temperature even if the marshmallow cream isn't fully toasted. True to its name, just one bite of this treat will leave you wanting "s'more."

FOR THE GRAHAM CRACKERS:

1 cup almond flour

½ cup coconut palm sugar,
plus more for sprinkling

1 tablespoon ground flaxseed

½ teaspoon ground cinnamon,
plus more for sprinkling

¼ teaspoon sea salt

Dash freshly ground nutmeg

1 tablespoon unrefined virgin
coconut oil, melted

½ teaspoon pure vanilla extract
or powder

FOR THE MARSHMALLOW CREAM:

One 13.5-ounce can full-fat
coconut milk, chilled

½ teaspoon pure vanilla extract
or powder

1 tablespoon raw honey or
pure maple syrup

(1) Position a rack in the middle of the oven and preheat to 350°F. Line a rimmed baking sheet with parchment paper. Set aside.

(2) **Make the graham crackers:** In a medium bowl, whisk together the flour, sugar, flaxseed, cinnamon, salt, and nutmeg. Stir in the coconut oil and vanilla. Add 2 tablespoons of water and stir until the mixture is completely moistened. Using your hands, bring the mixture together to form a ball. Transfer the dough to the prepared baking sheet and, using your hands, shape the dough into a 9-inch, ¼-inch-thick square. Sprinkle it with cinnamon and sugar and bake for 12 minutes, or until the bottom is slightly brown and the top springs back slightly when pressed. Let the cracker cool completely on the baking sheet.

(3) **Make the marshmallow cream:** Carefully open the can of chilled coconut milk and spoon the solids into a bowl (you can use the liquid at another time for baking or smoothies). Add the vanilla and honey and whisk vigorously until light and fluffy.

recipe and ingredients continue

TO ASSEMBLE:

Four 3-inch squares Favorite Freezer Chocolate Bar (page 35) or store-bought 72% or darker raw chocolate bar

1 to 2 tablespoons coconut or maple sugar

Refrigerate it until you're ready to assemble the s'mores.

4 **Assemble the s'mores:** Cut the cracker into nine 3-inch squares. Top four of the squares with a chocolate square and a dollop of the marshmallow cream. Sprinkle each with ¼ to ½ tablespoon of sugar and heat with a flame until slightly golden. Top with a second graham cracker (you'll have one cracker left over) and serve immediately.

dulce de leche sandwich cookies

MAKES FIVE 2½-INCH SANDWICH COOKIES

Ky lived in Argentina for a spell, where bakeries are known for their *alfajo-res*, a popular caramel sandwich cookie. These cookies are one of our more time-consuming recipes, but they're well worth the effort. Instead of using condensed milk, which is traditionally used to make dulce de leche, we boil coconut sugar and coconut cream to achieve a similar caramel flavor, and add cashew butter to enhance the texture. We sandwich a layer of our dulce de leche between two home-made cookies, then dip the whole thing in chocolate to create a truly decadent treat.

FOR THE DULCE DE LECHE:

1 cup coconut cream

1 cup coconut palm sugar

1 teaspoon pure vanilla extract or powder

¼ teaspoon sea salt

¼ cup creamy cashew butter

FOR THE COOKIES:

2 cups almond flour, plus more to dust the work surface

1 tablespoon coconut flour

¼ cup coconut palm sugar

1 tablespoon unrefined virgin coconut oil, melted

2 tablespoons non-dairy milk

¼ teaspoon sea salt

FOR THE CHOCOLATE SAUCE:

½ cup unrefined virgin coconut oil

1 tablespoon coconut butter

½ cup raw cacao powder

2 tablespoons pure maple syrup

① **Make the dulce de leche:** In a small saucepan over medium-high heat, bring the coconut cream and sugar to a boil. Reduce the heat and let simmer for 10 minutes, stirring constantly and being careful not to let the mixture boil over or burn on the bottom. The mixture will become thick and should coat the back of a spoon. Transfer the dulce de leche to a bowl, stir in the vanilla and salt, and place in the refrigerator to cool. It may seem thin at this point, but it will thicken when you add the cashew butter later.

② **Make the cookies:** Position a rack in the middle of the oven and preheat to 350°F. Line a baking sheet with parchment paper. Set aside.

③ In a large bowl, place the flours, sugar, coconut oil, milk, and salt and stir well to combine. The mixture will be crumbly. Using your hands, squeeze the mixture together until a dough forms. The dough becomes stickier as you work with it. If it's still crumbly, squeeze it a few more times; if it feels dry, add 1 teaspoon of water.

recipe continues

prep note • You can replace the chocolate sauce with 4 ounces of melted dark chocolate. For the coconut cream, you can buy it in a can or scoop the solids from 1 to 2 cans of coconut milk that have been refrigerated overnight; try not to tip or shake the can, as you want the solids to separate from the liquid.

Transfer the ball of dough to a surface lightly dusted with almond flour and roll it out to ¼-inch thickness. Using a 2½-inch round cookie cutter, cut out cookies. Gather any scraps and roll out the remaining dough, continuing to cut cookies and repeating until all the dough is used. You'll get about 10 cookies. Transfer the cookie cutouts to the prepared baking sheet, placing them about an inch or so apart, and bake for 8 to 10 minutes, until the bottoms and edges are slightly brown. Let them cool completely on the baking sheet.

4. **Make the chocolate sauce:** In a small saucepan over low heat, melt the coconut oil and butter together. Remove from the heat and add the cacao powder and maple syrup, whisking until smooth and fully combined. Allow the sauce to cool to room temperature.

5. **Assemble the cookies:** Set a wire rack over a sheet of parchment paper. Add the cashew butter to the chilled dulce de leche, stir until smooth, then chill in the freezer for 10 minutes. The caramel should be pliable and spreadable but still thick. If it's not, put it in the freezer for 10 more minutes until it holds its form.

6. Spread a generous layer of dulce de leche onto half of the cookies and top with the remaining cookies to make sandwiches. Using tongs, dip a cookie into the chocolate to cover it completely and place it on the wire rack. Or, conversely, lower the cookies into the chocolate using a fork. Repeat until all the cookies are covered, then transfer to the freezer to set the chocolate. If you have any chocolate sauce left over, give the cookies a second coat and freeze to set. Store the cookies in an airtight container in the refrigerator for up to 10 days.

sugar cookies with chocolate spread

MAKES 10 TO 12 COOKIES

Making sugar cookies has never been so easy—just stir the ingredients together and you'll be cutting out cookies in minutes. We originally made this cookie in the shape of a witch for our shop at Halloween, but you can make these for any occasion by using different shaped cookie cutters. We sold this limited edition for only three weeks, but our customers still ask for this cookie years later.

2 cups almond flour, plus more to dust the work surface

½ cup coconut palm sugar

½ teaspoon baking powder

Pinch sea salt

¼ cup unrefined virgin coconut oil, melted

½ teaspoon pure vanilla extract or powder

1 cup Original Chocolate Spread (page 42)

prep note • You can also shape the cookies by hand into small disks by forming them into balls, then flattening them on the sheet using the back of a spatula or even your hand.

1. Position a rack in the middle of the oven and preheat to 350°F. Line a rimmed baking sheet with parchment paper and set aside.

2. In a large bowl, whisk together the flour, sugar, baking powder, and salt until well combined. Add the coconut oil, vanilla, and 4½ teaspoons of water and stir well to combine. Form the dough into a ball.

3. Roll the cookie dough out on a lightly floured surface to ¼-inch thickness and cut out shapes using 3-inch cookie cutters. If the dough is difficult to roll out, use damp hands to lightly press it into an even round before cutting out the cookies. Reroll the dough scraps and continue cutting out cookies until all the dough is used.

4. Place the cookie cutouts on the prepared baking sheet about an inch or so apart and bake for 10 minutes, or until golden brown. Let the cookies cool fully on the baking sheet before frosting, about 30 minutes.

5. When cool, spread a layer of chocolate spread on top of each cookie. Store the cookies at room temperature in an airtight container for up to 5 days.

peanut butter & jelly sandwich cookies

MAKES 3 SANDWICH COOKIES

Bennett loves sandwich cookies. For a while she was sandwiching every spread imaginable, but peanut butter and jelly was her favorite combination. She took these classic flavors to new heights by spreading them between chocolate shortbread cookies, which are somewhat plain because really, they're just a vehicle for the creamy, gooey center. A cold glass of milk is the perfect accompaniment to this sweet-tasting sandwich.

1 cup all-purpose gluten-free flour

6 tablespoons coconut flour

¼ cup raw cacao powder

¼ teaspoon sea salt

⅓ cup coconut palm sugar

½ cup unrefined virgin coconut oil, melted

½ teaspoon pure vanilla extract or powder

2 tablespoons peanut butter

2 tablespoons jelly

1. Position a rack in the middle of the oven and preheat to 325°F. Line a rimmed baking sheet with parchment paper and set aside.

2. In a medium bowl, combine the flours, cacao powder, and salt. In another bowl, stir together the sugar, coconut oil, and vanilla and incorporate into the flour mixture. Stir until thoroughly combined or use your hands to knead the dough. Using your hands, divide the dough into 6 portions, roll into balls, and place the balls on the prepared baking sheet about 2 inches apart. Flatten with your hand to make 2-inch rounds. Bake for 12 minutes, or until slightly golden.

3. Let the cookies cool completely on the baking sheet, then transfer to a plate. Spread 2 teaspoons of peanut butter on half of the cookies and spread 2 teaspoons of jelly on the remaining cookies. Press one peanut butter and one jelly cookie together to make a sandwich. Repeat with the remaining cookies. Store in an airtight container at room temperature for 1 to 2 days.

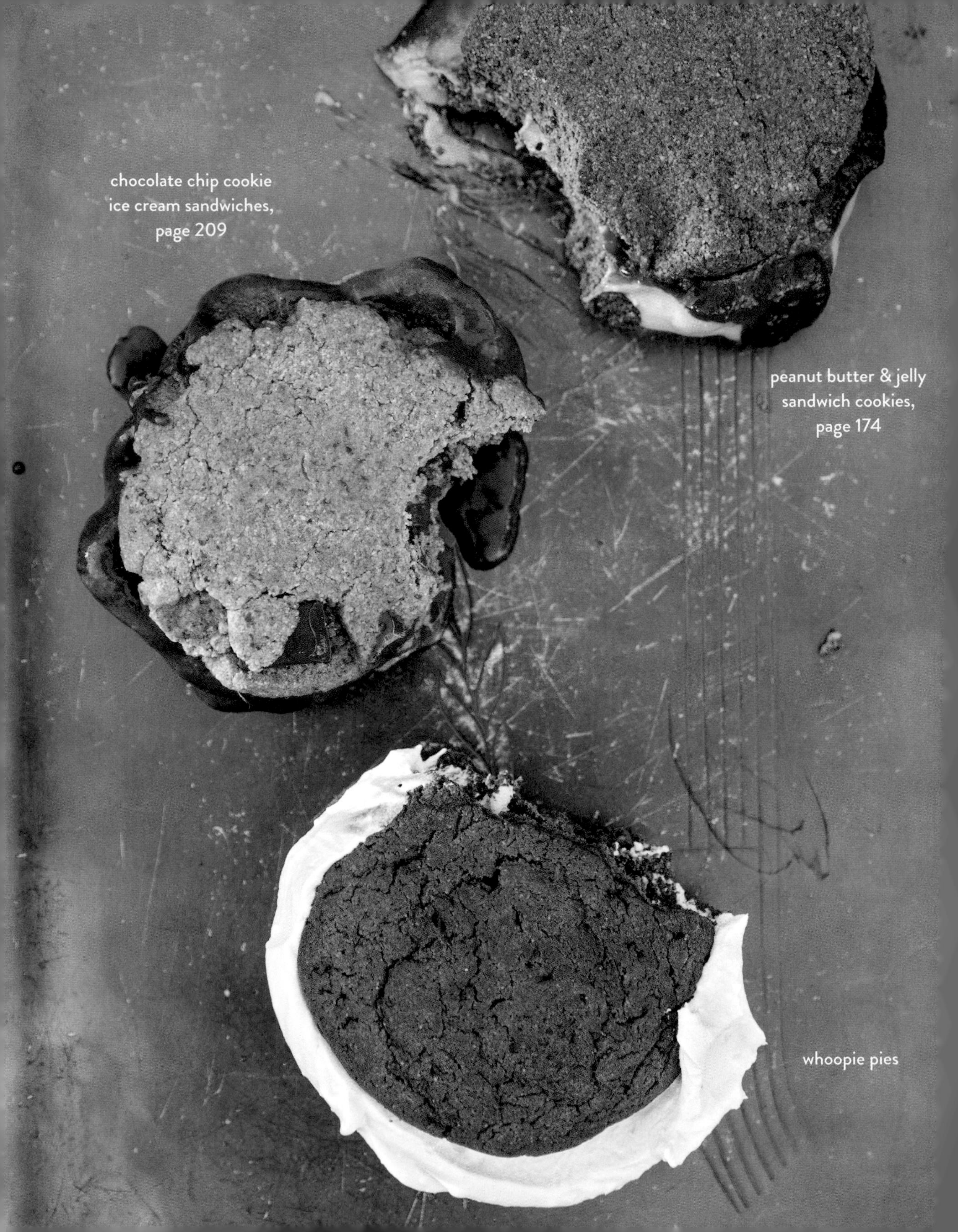

chocolate chip cookie
ice cream sandwiches,
page 209

peanut butter & jelly
sandwich cookies,
page 174

whoopie pies

whoopie pies

MAKES 6 PIES

We've never figured out if whoopie pies should be classified as cookies or cakes, so we like to call them sweet sandwiches instead. These soft, cakey cookies are a New England specialty. As with so many recipes, we've given this classic our own twist by making the cookies gluten-free and replacing the traditional center of icing or marshmallow fluff with a big spoonful of fluffy coconut cream.

1 cup coconut palm sugar

½ cup raw cacao powder

½ cup unrefined virgin coconut oil, melted

1 teaspoon pure vanilla extract or powder

1 teaspoon baking powder

¾ teaspoon sea salt

½ teaspoon baking soda

1 Flax Egg (page 47)

1 cup full-fat coconut milk, can shaken or stirred well to recombine

2⅓ cups gluten-free all-purpose flour

1½ to 2 cups Coconut Whipped Cream (page 44)

1. Position a rack in the middle of the oven and preheat to 350°F. Line two baking sheets with parchment paper and set aside.

2. In a medium bowl, stir together the sugar, cacao powder, coconut oil, vanilla, baking powder, salt, and baking soda. Beat in the flax egg. Slowly stir in the coconut milk, followed by the flour. Mix until well combined. Scoop twelve 2-tablespoon-size mounds onto the prepared baking sheet, placing them about 4 inches apart (the cookies will spread). Using your hand, flatten the cookies to make 3-inch rounds. Bake for 15 minutes, or until they spring back lightly to the touch. Let the cookies cool completely on the baking sheet.

3. Spread the coconut whipped cream over half of the cookies and top with the remaining cookies. Serve immediately.

chocolate caramel popcorn

MAKES 6 CUPS

Crunchy and sweet, this popcorn will take movie night to new heights. Coconut sugar has a natural toffee flavor that, combined with sunflower seed butter, makes a deliciously nutty caramel sauce. After the popcorn is coated and baked, it gets wonderfully crispy and is finished with a dark chocolate drizzle.

FOR THE POPCORN:

1 tablespoon coconut or olive oil

⅓ cup popcorn kernels

FOR THE CARAMEL SAUCE:

½ cup coconut palm sugar

3 tablespoons sunflower seed butter

2 tablespoons unrefined virgin coconut oil

½ teaspoon sea salt

FOR THE CHOCOLATE SAUCE:

¼ cup raw cacao butter, coarsely chopped

¼ cup raw cacao powder

1 tablespoon pure maple syrup

1. Position a rack in the center of the oven and preheat to 300°F. Line a baking sheet with parchment paper and set aside.

2. **Make the popcorn:** Add the coconut oil to a large stockpot over high heat, then add the popcorn kernels and cover. After you hear the first kernel pop, shake the pot back and forth over the burner for 3 to 4 minutes, until you hear very few to no kernels popping anymore. Remove from the heat and carefully remove the lid, allowing the steam to escape. Reserve 6 cups of the popcorn and set aside. Save the rest for another use.

3. **Make the caramel sauce:** Bring the sugar and 2 tablespoons of water to a boil in a small saucepan. Boil for 45 seconds, or until the mixture thickens slightly. Remove from the heat and whisk in the sunflower seed butter, coconut oil, and salt until smooth. The consistency will be thin. If the mixture is too thick, add 1 tablespoon of water.

prep note • We prefer home-popped corn to the commercial type you pop in the microwave, of which the latter is extremely salty and usually doused in some type of artificial flavorings. To pop popcorn on the stovetop, pour 1 tablespoon of coconut or olive oil in the bottom of a large pot, then add ⅓ cup of popcorn kernels, which will yield 6 to 8 cups of popped corn. Cover and set over high heat until you hear one kernel pop then begin to shake the pot back and forth over the flame or burner for 3 to 4 minutes, until you no longer hear any, or just a few kernels popping. Remove from the heat and carefully remove the lid, allowing the steam to escape, and use the popcorn as desired.

④ Drizzle the sauce over the popcorn then, using two spoons, toss to coat. Spread the caramel corn in a single layer on the prepared pan. Bake for 10 minutes, or until the edges are crispy, stirring once halfway through the baking.

⑤ **While the popcorn bakes, make the chocolate sauce:** In a small saucepan over low heat, cook the cacao butter until fully melted. Remove from the heat and whisk in the cacao powder and maple syrup until smooth and fully combined.

⑥ Immediately drizzle the chocolate sauce over the baked popcorn and transfer to the refrigerator for a few minutes to set. Store in an airtight container at room temperature for 2 to 3 days.

pineapple "doughnuts"

MAKES 9 DOUGHNUTS

Pineapple is undoubtedly delicious, and it's a nutritional powerhouse high in vitamin C, folate, and fiber. But we confess: in this recipe we just use it as a vehicle to deliver chocolate and our beloved coconut bacon, which we serve in our shop regularly. It may come as a surprise, but tossing coconut flakes with smoked paprika and smoked maple syrup is suggestive of bacon. The combination of sweet pineapple, bitter chocolate, and smoky coconut bacon may seem unexpected, but it really works.

FOR THE "BACON":

1 tablespoon smoked maple syrup (see Prep Note, page 182) or pure maple syrup

1 tablespoon smoked paprika

1 tablespoon coconut aminos

½ teaspoon sea salt or smoked sea salt

Pinch freshly ground black pepper

1 cup coconut flakes

FOR THE "DOUGHNUTS":

1 whole pineapple

FOR THE CHOCOLATE COATING:

½ cup raw cacao butter, coarsely chopped

½ cup coconut butter

¾ cup pure maple syrup

⅔ cup raw cacao powder

1 teaspoon pure vanilla extract or powder

① Position a rack in the middle of the oven and preheat to 325°F. Line a baking sheet with parchment paper and set aside.

② **Make the coconut bacon:** In a medium bowl, whisk together the maple syrup, paprika, aminos, salt, and pepper. Add the coconut and stir to coat. Spread the coconut in a single layer on the prepared baking sheet. Toast for 12 minutes, stirring halfway through the baking time, until the coconut is slightly dry and begins to brown at the edges. Let the bacon cool on the pan. It will turn crunchy once it cools.

③ **Prepare the pineapple doughnuts:** Place a wire rack over a baking sheet lined with parchment paper. Set aside.

④ Cut off the top and bottom of the pineapple. Stand the pineapple on its end and cut away the skin. Slice the pineapple into ¼-inch slices. Using a small knife or round cookie cutter, cut out the center core of each slice.

recipe continues

prep note • Smoked maple syrup is worth seeking out. Just a drizzle gives foods a wonderful smoky sweetness. We like to use Sugar Bob's Finest Kind Smoked Maple Syrup, which is available online.

⑤ **Make the chocolate coating:** In a small saucepan over low heat, melt together the cacao and coconut butters. Remove from the heat and whisk in the maple syrup, cacao powder, and vanilla until smooth and fully combined.

⑥ Dip each pineapple slice completely into the chocolate coating and place on the prepared rack. Sprinkle with the coconut bacon. Put the doughnuts with the rack and baking sheet in the refrigerator to chill for 20 minutes. Enjoy immediately.

tiramisu

MAKES ONE 8 X 8-INCH CAKE

The combination of flavors and textures makes this one decadent dessert that is beloved by many—it is hands down one of our best sellers at the shop. We make a homemade mascarpone with macadamia and cashew nuts and coconut milk to create a fluffy, light cream to layer between our espresso-soaked vanilla cake. This dessert is so irresistible you may have the urge to dig in right away, but it's best to let it set overnight so the flavors can mingle and deepen.

FOR THE CAKE:

½ cup coconut flour

½ cup oat flour

1 teaspoon baking powder

1 teaspoon baking soda

1 teaspoon sea salt

¾ cup pure maple syrup

⅓ cup unrefined virgin coconut oil, melted

2 tablespoons apple cider vinegar

2 teaspoons pure vanilla powder or extract

FOR THE MASCARPONE:

One 13.5-ounce can full-fat coconut milk

1 cup raw cashews

1 cup raw macadamia nuts

½ cup unrefined virgin coconut oil

⅓ cup pure maple syrup

2 teaspoons pure vanilla powder or extract

¼ teaspoon sea salt

1. **Make the cake:** Position a rack in the center of the oven and preheat to 350°F. Line a baking sheet with parchment paper and set aside.

2. In a large bowl, whisk together the flours, baking powder, baking soda, and salt. In a medium bowl, stir the maple syrup, coconut oil, vinegar, and vanilla together with ⅔ cup of warm water. Add the wet ingredients to the dry and whisk to combine until no lumps remain.

3. Spread the batter onto the prepared baking sheet in an 8 x 16-inch rectangle that's ¼ inch thick. Bake for 20 minutes, or until the edges turn dark golden and the top just begins to crack. Let the cake cool on the baking sheet for 20 minutes, then transfer to the freezer for 10 minutes.

4. **While the cake cools, prepare the mascarpone:** In a high-speed blender, puree the coconut milk, cashews, macadamia nuts, coconut oil, maple syrup, vanilla, and salt until creamy.

recipe and ingredients continue

TO ASSEMBLE:

1 cup chilled espresso or strong coffee

¼ cup raw cacao powder

prep note • You could also use little jars to make individual desserts; these will require less time to set.

⑤ **Assemble the cake:** Cut the chilled cake in half crosswise and place one piece in an 8 x 8-inch dish (see Prep Note). Keep the other half in the freezer. Pour ½ cup of the espresso over the cake, then spread half of the mascarpone in an even layer over the espresso. Transfer to the refrigerator for 20 minutes, or until set.

⑥ Using a fine-mesh strainer, dust the mascarpone layer with 2 tablespoons of the cacao powder and place the second cake layer on top. Soak with the remaining ½ cup espresso and spread with the remaining mascarpone, then chill for 20 minutes. Dust the top layer with the remaining 2 tablespoons cacao powder. Cover with plastic wrap and chill in the refrigerator overnight to fully set, then store leftovers in the refrigerator for up to 4 days.

chocolate tart
with mashed raspberries and pine nut crust

MAKES ONE 8-INCH SQUARE TART

There is something romantic about the pairing of raspberries and chocolate—they're a match made in heaven. The striking red berries against the dark chocolate ganache make this a beautiful and showstopping dessert. And the pine nut crust—it's so rich and buttery, we think it tastes exactly like shortbread. This tart will make anyone feel loved.

FOR THE CRUST:

3 tablespoons unrefined virgin coconut oil, plus more for greasing the pan

2 cups almond flour

1½ cups pine nuts

¾ cup unsweetened shredded coconut

3 tablespoons pure maple syrup

¾ teaspoon pure vanilla extract or powder

¾ teaspoon sea salt

FOR THE RASPBERRY LAYER:

2 cups fresh red raspberries

FOR THE DARK CHOCOLATE GANACHE:

1 cup pure maple syrup

½ cup unrefined virgin coconut oil

1 cup raw cacao powder

1 tablespoon pure vanilla extract or powder (optional)

½ teaspoon sea salt (optional)

1 cup fresh red raspberries, for serving

① Position a rack in the middle of the oven and preheat to 350°F. Grease an 8 x 8-inch square tart pan with a removable bottom and set aside.

② **Make the crust:** Combine the coconut oil, flour, pine nuts, coconut, maple syrup, vanilla, and salt in a food processor and run until a dough forms.

③ Press the dough evenly onto the bottom and up the sides of the prepared tart pan. Prick the bottom of the crust with a fork. Bake for 10 to 12 minutes, until lightly golden. Let the crust cool completely in the pan, about 1 hour.

④ **Make the raspberry layer:** Add the raspberries to a medium bowl and mash gently with a fork. Spread the mashed berries over the cooled crust and set aside.

⑤ **Make the dark chocolate ganache:** In a blender, puree the maple syrup and coconut oil until combined. Add the cacao powder and the vanilla and salt, if using, and blend again until smooth. Pour the filling evenly over the mashed raspberry layer. Chill the tart in the refrigerator until firm, about 30 minutes. Artfully arrange the remaining 1 cup of raspberries over the ganache layer before serving. Store the tart covered in the refrigerator for up to 3 days.

crunchy salty peanut butter chocolate tart

MAKES ONE 14 X 4-INCH TART

This is an impressive dessert to take to a party because, unlike other tarts that may be messy to serve, this one has a thick peanut butter and oat crust that holds its shape. A dark chocolate filling and a sprinkling of flaky salt bring it over the top. We usually cut the tart into bars, but it can also be cut into triangle wedges and eaten like a New York–style slice (of pizza, that is!).

FOR THE CRUST:

6 tablespoons unrefined virgin coconut oil, melted, plus more for greasing the pan

1½ cups oat flour

1 cup old-fashioned rolled oats

⅔ cup coconut palm sugar

1 teaspoon sea salt

½ cup crunchy peanut butter

2 tablespoons almond milk

FOR THE CHOCOLATE FILLING:

½ cup pure maple syrup

½ cup coconut cream

1 cup raw cacao powder

1 tablespoon flaky sea salt

1. Position a rack in the middle of the oven and preheat to 350°F. Grease a 14 x 4-inch rectangular tart pan with a removable bottom with oil. Set aside.

2. **Make the crust:** In a large bowl, stir together the oat flour, oats, sugar, and salt. Add the coconut oil, peanut butter, and almond milk and stir well to combine. The dough should be thick and sticky. Turn the dough out into the tart pan and press evenly along the bottom and up the sides. The crust should be thick.

3. Prick the bottom of the crust with a fork and bake for 15 minutes, or until slightly brown and toasty. Set aside to cool.

4. **While the crust cools, make the chocolate filling:** Warm the maple syrup in a small saucepan over medium heat. Whisk in the coconut cream, then add the cacao powder and whisk until smooth. Pour the mixture into the cooled crust and refrigerate for 1 hour, or until firm. Sprinkle with the salt before serving. Store the tart at room temperature for up to 3 days.

chocolate cream pie

MAKES ONE 9-INCH PIE

Our chocolate cream pie will conjure up that dessert case loaded with pies, layer cakes, and maybe a few Jell-O cups at an old-fashioned diner. The difference between their cream pie and ours? We don't use Cool Whip! Instead we slather coconut cream over a silky-smooth chocolate pudding filling made from nut and cacao butters and high-quality chocolate. Free of wheat, dairy, and preservatives, this pie is quite literally just naturally delicious!

FOR THE CRUST:

2 cups almond flour

2 tablespoons coconut palm sugar

3 tablespoons unrefined virgin coconut oil, melted

2 tablespoons almond milk

Pinch sea salt

FOR THE CHOCOLATE CREAM FILLING:

One 13.5-ounce can full-fat coconut milk

⅓ cup almond or cashew butter

¼ cup raw cacao butter, coarsely chopped

5 ounces 72% or darker raw chocolate or Traditional Raw Chocolate Bar (page 34), chopped

½ cup pure maple syrup

1 teaspoon pure vanilla extract or powder

¼ teaspoon sea salt

2 to 3 cups Coconut Whipped Cream (page 44)

Shaved chocolate, for serving (optional)

1. Preheat the oven to 350°F.

2. **Make the crust:** In a medium bowl, whisk together the flour and sugar. Stir in the coconut oil, almond milk, and salt until well combined. Press the mixture into a 9-inch pie pan and bake for 12 minutes, or until it starts to turn the slightest golden color on the edges. Set the crust on a wire rack and let cool completely.

3. **While the crust cools, make the filling:** In a large saucepan over medium heat, combine the coconut milk and nut and cacao butters. Add the chopped chocolate and stir until fully melted.

4. Pour the mixture into a blender and add the maple syrup, vanilla, and salt. Puree until smooth. Pour the filling into the cooled crust and transfer to the refrigerator for about 1 hour, until the filling is firm to the touch.

5. Spread a thick coat of coconut whipped cream on top of the pie and garnish with shaved chocolate if desired. Store in the refrigerator covered for up to 2 days.

frozen goodness

Summer is when our shop really hops.
After all, the population of Martha's Vineyard
increases by a whopping 100,000 during high season!
We naturally ramp up production, especially for our
frozen drinks. Isn't that what vacation is all about—
smiling kids with sticky chins from melted ice
cream and sandy feet from a day at the beach?

black and white frappe

MAKES 2

You can enjoy some island summer fun any time of year with this New England favorite. Ky learned to make a mean black and white frappe (made with vanilla ice cream and chocolate syrup and considered a chocolate milkshake in the rest of the country) while working years ago at a popular breakfast spot in Martha's Vineyard. She has since created her own dairy-free version. Frappe or milkshake—maybe the best thing to call it is delicious.

1 cup coconut cream

¾ cup almond milk

½ cup raw macadamia nuts, preferably soaked overnight, then drained and rinsed

½ cup packed pitted dates

1 teaspoon pure vanilla extract or powder

2 cups ice

2 tablespoons Be Saucy Chocolate Sauce (page 38)

1. Add the coconut cream, almond milk, macadamia nuts, dates, and vanilla to a blender and blend until creamy. Add the ice and 1 tablespoon chocolate sauce and blend again.

2. Drizzle the remaining 1 tablespoon of chocolate sauce along the inside of two glasses. Divide the frappe between the glasses and serve immediately.

prep note • If you have leftover frappe, pour it in a popsicle mold and freeze. Let it thaw 10 minutes before eating.

peanut butter and strawberry ice cube tray chocolates

MAKES 12 CHOCOLATES

This is one of our favorite recipes for when we need chocolate *now*. The best time to make these treats is in late spring through early summer, when strawberries are at their ripest. Using fresh, succulent berries in these creamy peanut butter chocolates ensures every bite will be bursting with flavor. The juicier the strawberries, the better.

½ cup raw cacao butter, coarsely chopped

½ cup unrefined virgin coconut oil

1 cup raw cacao powder

¼ cup pure maple syrup or agave nectar

The seeds scraped from 1 whole vanilla bean or 1 teaspoon pure vanilla extract

¼ teaspoon sea salt

¼ cup peanut butter

6 fresh strawberries, hulled and thinly sliced

prep note • You can swap out the peanut butter and strawberries for any nut butter and fruit you like—the combinations are endless. We've made these with tahini and peaches, for example, and loved the results.

1. In a small saucepan over low heat, combine the cacao butter and coconut oil and cook until melted. Whisk in the cacao powder, maple syrup, vanilla, and salt.

2. Fill each cavity in a 12-ice cube tray with a generous teaspoonful of the chocolate sauce. Top each with 1 teaspoon of peanut butter and a few strawberry slices. Divide the remaining chocolate over the strawberry slices in each cavity.

3. Place the ice cube tray in the freezer and allow the chocolates to set for 15 minutes. When ready to eat, remove the tray from the freezer and let sit for a few minutes before removing from the tray and eating. Store in an airtight container in the refrigerator for up to 3 days.

fudgesicles

MAKES TEN 2.75-OUNCE POPS

This recipe happened purely by accident. One day, Ky froze leftover chocolate cheesecake filling into a popsicle mold to see what would happen and these fudge-sicles were born. The secret here is healthy fats, which make the fudgesicles light and creamy but also rich, with a slightly chewy texture, just like the ones you may remember from childhood.

One 13.5-ounce can full-fat coconut milk

1½ cups raw cashews, soaked in boiling water for 10 minutes then drained

¼ cup unrefined virgin coconut oil

¼ cup raw cacao powder

¼ cup raw cacao butter, melted

¼ cup pure maple syrup

Be Saucy Chocolate Sauce (page 38), coconut flakes, chopped pistachios, goji berries, or flaky sea salt, for serving (optional)

1. Add the coconut milk, soaked cashews, coconut oil, cacao powder, cacao butter, and maple syrup to a high-speed blender and puree until completely smooth.

2. Pour the mixture into ten 2.75-ounce popsicle molds and freeze until firm, about 4 hours. Drizzle with the chocolate sauce and sprinkle with your desired toppings just before serving.

avocado mousse
with pistachios and pomegranate

SERVES 4

This versatile recipe is tough to categorize; its puddinglike texture makes it seem like a decadent dessert, but because it's packed with whole foods that give you fiber, healthy fats, and antioxidants, it also works as a delicious breakfast or power snack. Whenever you serve it, it's a quick treat with rich chocolate flavor.

And when you're craving ice cream, reach for this instead. The cold, creamy texture is deeply satisfying.

1 cup pitted dates, soaked in boiling water for 10 minutes then drained

½ cup raw cashews, soaked in boiling water for 10 minutes then drained

One 13.5-ounce can full-fat coconut milk

1 small avocado, pitted, peeled, and cut into large chunks

½ cup raw cacao powder

Coconut Whipped Cream (page 44), pomegranate seeds, and chopped pistachios, for serving

(1) In a high-speed blender or food processor, combine the soaked dates and cashews, coconut milk, avocado, and cacao powder and blend until smooth. Divide the mousse among four 4-ounce serving cups or ramekins. Serve with a spoonful of coconut whipped cream and a sprinkling of pomegranate seeds and pistachios.

(2) You can store the mousse in the refrigerator, without toppings and covered, for 3 to 5 days, or in the freezer, covered in plastic wrap and in an airtight container, for up to 3 months.

prep note • This mousse also makes great popsicles.

instant soft serve ice cream
with chocolate magic shell

SERVES 4

We keep bananas and fruit stocked in our freezers for many reasons, but especially so we can make this ice cream in a matter of minutes. We're including two flavors here: black raspberry and peanut butter. Both pair nicely with Chocolate Magic Shell (page 37). Cracking the shell is so much fun, you might just feel like a kid all over again. For a sweet ending to a special meal, set up a toppings bar with cacao nibs, shredded coconut, chopped nuts, and your favorite toasted seeds.

FOR BLACK RASPBERRY:

2 frozen bananas, coarsely chopped

2 tablespoons non-dairy milk

1 cup frozen pitted cherries

½ cup frozen black raspberries, or blackberries, or more as needed

1 teaspoon pure vanilla extract or powder

FOR PEANUT BUTTER:

3 frozen bananas, coarsely chopped, or more as needed

⅓ cup peanut butter

TO ASSEMBLE:

1 recipe Chocolate Magic Shell (page 37)

Raw cacao nibs, shredded coconut, nuts, or seeds, for serving (optional)

① **Make the soft serve of your choice:** Combine your chosen variation's ingredients in a high-speed blender and puree on high until smooth and creamy. If the ice cream is runny, add more frozen fruit, and conversely if it's hard to process, add a little liquid at a time. (You can use a little non-dairy milk for the Peanut Butter Soft Serve if needed.)

② **Assemble:** Scoop the ice cream into bowls. If your ice cream isn't super cold, put it in the freezer until it holds its shape in a spoon. Pour the magic shell on top and sprinkle with your desired toppings. Place the bowl in the freezer for 30 seconds to harden the shell and serve immediately.

golden milk ice cream
with chocolate chips

SERVES 4

Golden milk is a traditional Ayurvedic recipe made from turmeric, spices, and coconut milk, typically served warm and prized for its anti-inflammatory properties. Its ingredients are naturally synergistic: the fat in the coconut milk aids in the absorption of the fat-soluble vitamin E, and the black pepper enhances the turmeric's potency by making the curcumin more bioavailable. We've turned this prized ancient drink into ice cream and added our own modern twist: homemade chocolate chips.

FOR THE ICE CREAM:

One 13.5-ounce can full-fat coconut milk

One 2-inch piece fresh ginger, peeled

2 teaspoons ground turmeric

½ teaspoon ground cinnamon

⅛ teaspoon freshly ground black pepper

Pinch sea salt

1 cup raw cashews

¼ cup pure maple syrup

1 teaspoon pure vanilla extract

FOR THE CHOCOLATE CHIPS:

¼ cup unrefined virgin coconut oil

¼ heaping cup raw cacao powder

¼ cup pure maple syrup

1. **Make the ice cream base:** In a medium saucepan over low heat, combine the coconut milk, ginger, turmeric, cinnamon, black pepper, and salt and bring to a simmer. Remove the milk from the heat and refrigerate overnight.

2. **The next day, make the chocolate chips:** Line a baking sheet with parchment paper and set aside.

3. In a small saucepan over medium heat, heat the coconut oil until fully melted, then reduce the heat and whisk in the cacao powder and maple syrup until smooth. Pour the chocolate onto the prepared baking sheet and spread it in a thin layer. Immediately transfer the baking sheet to the freezer for about 15 minutes, until the chocolate is firm.

4. To finish the ice cream, strain the chilled ice cream base, discarding the ginger, and pour into a high-speed blender. Add the cashews, maple syrup, and vanilla and puree on high until smooth.

⑤ Transfer the mixture to an ice cream machine and freeze according to the manufacturer's instructions. Break the chocolate into small pieces and fold it into the ice cream. Transfer the ice cream to a freezer-safe container and chill another hour to firm if desired or up to 1 week. Otherwise, serve immediately.

frozen bonbons

We like to make these bonbons with strawberries and banana, but you can use any frozen fruit you have on hand. We keep a container of these in the freezer all summer, especially to satisfy our after-dinner cravings for a little something sweet.

1 cup frozen strawberries

1 frozen banana

1 tablespoon coconut cream

1 tablespoon raw honey

4 ounces 72% or darker raw chocolate or Traditional Raw Chocolate Bar (page 34), chopped

1. Add the strawberries, banana, coconut cream, and honey to a high-speed blender and puree until smooth.

2. Scrape the mixture into a covered container and freeze overnight, or until firm.

3. The next day, melt the chocolate in a small saucepan over low heat and let it cool to the touch.

4. Place a wire rack over a baking sheet lined with parchment paper and scoop the frozen fruit filling into large tablespoon-size balls, working quickly and placing the balls on the prepared rack. You may have to shape them with your hands. Pour the chocolate over the balls and put the baking sheet in the freezer for 30 to 45 minutes, or until the balls are firm. Serve immediately or store the bonbons in an airtight container in the freezer for up to 2 weeks.

chocolate chip cookie ice cream sandwiches

MAKES 6 SANDWICHES

You know when you get the urge to grab one of those packaged ice cream sandwiches at a gas station or grocery store? Next time that happens, make these: they're the version that your body really wants. We make our own ice cream using banana, chocolate, and peanut butter, then sandwich it between soft homemade cookies. To make these even easier, you could use your favorite non-dairy vanilla ice cream instead. If you want to skip the ice cream altogether, these cookies are excellent on their own or with an ice-cold glass of milk.

FOR THE ICE CREAM:

- 2 frozen bananas, coarsely chopped
- ¼ cup raw cacao powder
- 2 tablespoons almond milk
- 1 tablespoon peanut butter or nut butter of your choice
- 1 tablespoon raw honey

FOR THE COOKIES:

- 1½ cups oat flour
- ½ cup old-fashioned rolled oats
- ¼ cup coconut palm sugar
- ½ teaspoon baking soda
- ⅓ teaspoon baking powder
- ¼ teaspoon sea salt
- ½ cup chopped 72% or darker raw chocolate or chocolate chips

1. **Make the ice cream:** Add all the ingredients to a high-speed blender and puree for about 20 seconds, until smooth; the mixture will have the consistency of a thick cream. Pour the mixture into a covered freezer-safe container and freeze for about 1 hour, until it has a firmer ice cream–like texture

2. **While the ice cream freezes, make the cookies:** Position a rack in the middle of the oven and preheat to 350°F. Line a baking sheet with parchment paper and set aside.

3. In a large mixing bowl, whisk together the oat flour, oats, sugar, baking soda, baking powder, and salt, then stir in the chopped chocolate.

4. In a small bowl, whisk together the chia eggs, maple syrup, coconut oil, and vanilla until fully

recipe and ingredients continue

2 Chia Eggs (page 47)

¼ cup pure maple syrup

¼ cup unrefined virgin coconut
   oil, melted

1 teaspoon pure vanilla extract
   or powder

incorporated. Add the wet ingredients to the dry and stir until well combined. The dough will seem dry, so keep stirring until all the ingredients are moist and incorporated.

⑤ Using two heaping tablespoons of dough, form balls and place them on the prepared baking sheet 2 inches apart, pressing them down slightly with an offset spatula to flatten, until they're about 2½ inches wide. Bake for 12 minutes, or until the cookies crack on top. Allow the cookies to cool completely on the baking sheet.

⑥ **Assemble the sandwiches:** Place one large scoop of ice cream between two cookies and press together. If the ice cream is runny, freeze them for at least 30 minutes or until it firms slightly. Store in an airtight container in the freezer for up to 1 week.

peanut butter & jelly
sandwich cookies, page 174

chocolate chip cookie
ice cream sandwiches

whoopie pies,
page 177

cookies and cream no-churn ice cream cake

SERVES 6 TO 8

When it's really hot, the last thing we want to do is turn on the oven—we'd rather be at the beach than in the kitchen! So when we need a special dessert for a summer celebration, this ice cream cake is what we make. All you need is a blender to create layers of ice cream. We use raw cacao nibs to create chocolatey cookie crumbles that are rich with antioxidants and deliciously crunchy.

FOR THE CHOCOLATE COOKIE LAYERS:

3 cups almond or oat flour

1½ cups raw cacao nibs

6 tablespoons raw cacao powder

2 tablespoons pure maple syrup

2 tablespoons coconut palm sugar

FOR THE ICE CREAM LAYERS:

1½ cups raw cashews, soaked for 10 minutes in hot water then drained

One 13.5-ounce can full-fat coconut milk

¼ cup unrefined virgin coconut oil, melted and cooled

6 tablespoons pure maple syrup

¼ cup raw cacao butter, melted and cooled

2 teaspoons pure vanilla powder or extract

1 recipe Chocolate Magic Shell, for serving (page 37; optional)

① Line a 9 x 5-inch loaf pan with parchment paper, leaving an overhang on two opposite sides. Set aside.

② **Make the chocolate cookie:** In a large bowl, stir together the flour, cacao nibs, cacao powder, maple syrup, and sugar. Add 2 tablespoons of water and continue stirring. The mixture will be crumbly and will not form a dough, but should stick together when you pinch a small amount in your fingers. If it's not coming together, add 1 to 2 more tablespoons of water. Transfer half of the cookie mixture to the pan and, using your hands, gently press it into the bottom. Place the pan in the freezer for 10 minutes. Set the other half of the cookie mixture aside.

③ **Make the ice cream:** Add the soaked cashews, coconut milk, coconut oil, maple syrup, cacao butter, and vanilla to a high-speed blender and puree until very smooth and creamy, scraping

recipe continues

down the sides as needed, 2 to 3 minutes. Pour half of the mixture into the loaf pan to cover the cookie layer. Return the pan to the freezer for 1 hour, or until firm. Refrigerate the remaining ice cream mixture.

4. Sprinkle the remaining cookie mixture over the firm ice cream layer, then gently pour the remaining ice cream on top. Place the cake in the freezer until completely set, 6 to 8 hours, or overnight.

5. When the ice cream cake is frozen, run a knife along the edges of the cake and invert the loaf pan onto a plate. Unmold the cake with a good tap. If the ice cream cake is too hard and isn't coming out easily, let it warm up for 5 to 10 minutes so that it releases from the pan. Top with chocolate magic shell sauce if desired. Serve immediately.

watermelon and chocolate seed pops

MAKES FOUR TO SIX 2.75-OUNCE POPSICLES

Designed for hot summer days, these icy pops are exactly what you want to quench your thirst after a long day of paddleboarding or swimming in the sun. Watermelon contains an amino acid called L-citrulline, which can help relax sore muscles—exactly what you want after a day of physical activity. But you don't need exercise to enjoy these chilly, energizing treats; they're delicious either way!

FOR THE CHOCOLATE CHIPS:
¼ cup unrefined virgin coconut oil
¼ heaping cup raw cacao powder
¼ cup pure maple syrup

FOR THE WATERMELON FILLING:
2 cups cubed seedless watermelon
1 cup sliced fresh strawberries

① Line a baking sheet with parchment paper and set aside.

② **Make the chocolate chips:** In a small saucepan over low heat, cook the coconut oil until melted. Whisk in the cacao powder and maple syrup until smooth. Pour the chocolate onto the baking sheet, spreading it in a thin layer with a spatula, then place it in the freezer to firm, about 30 minutes.

③ **Make the watermelon filling:** Add the watermelon and strawberries to a high-speed blender and puree until smooth. Pour the mixture into popsicle molds, filling them halfway.

④ Remove the chocolate from the freezer and break it into small, chip-size pieces. Divide the chocolate chips among the popsicle molds, then top with the remaining filling. Insert a popsicle stick into each mold, then place in the freezer to firm, 30 to 40 minutes.

acknowledgments

To the community of Martha's Vineyard, our loyal customers, and anyone who has bought one of our products. You gave us the encouragement and confidence to grow this beyond a tiny seed of an idea. Because of you, we dared pursue this further, open our shop, and write this book. Your feedback, cheering comments, and purchase of our products helped us improve our chocolate and grow our recipes.

We thank our amazing staff at Not Your Sugar Mamas—especially Jamie Cekala, who is the glue that keeps NYSM together; Erica McIntosh for all that you do; and Alex, Elizabeth, and our staff members past, present, and future who put your hard work and dedication into NYSM. We are so grateful and humbled by all of you.

Thanks to our beloved families for your support of this idea and its growth every step of the way. We appreciate your encouragement to pursue our dreams. We love you. Special shout out to Bennett's parents for letting us use their kitchen as NYSM "headquarters" in our humble beginnings.

Thanks to Sophie for believing in us and seeing our potential before we did. Thanks to Craig for your kindness and generosity of support.

To Elizabeth Cecil for her genius. Special thanks to Sarah Waldman, Angela Miller, and Rebecca Miller Ffrench for making this book possible.

To our taste testers, especially the Counter family (Chris in particular) and Wolfie, thanks for eating every little thing that came out of the kitchen, good or bad.

A special thanks from Ky to Francesca (Frankie) for being my motivation to create healthier food for you and the planet. And to my best friend, Amy Leshner, for helping me watch her so I could shoot the book. :)

And from Bennett to Wolfie, August, and Charlie for giving me more love than I could ever have imagined. It's my reason for everything.

notes

Introduction

1 Elizabeth Mostofsky et al., "Chocolate Intake and Risk of Clinically Apparent Atrial Fibrillation: The Danish Diet, Cancer, and Health Study," *Heart* 103 (2017): 1163–67.

2 Francene M. Steinberg, Monica M. Bearden, and Carl L. Keen, "Cocoa and Chocolate Flavonoids: Implications for Cardiovascular Health," *Journal of the American Dietetic Association* 103, no. 2 (2003): 215–23. L. H. Yao et al., "Flavonoids in Food and Their Health Benefits," *Plant Foods for Human Nutrition* 59, no. 3 (2004): 113–22.

3 Whitney Leigh Harrington, "The Effects of Roasting Time and Temperature on the Antioxidant Capacity of Cocoa Beans from Dominican Republic, Ecuador, Haiti, Indonesia, and Ivory Coast" (master's thesis, University of Tennessee, 2011).

Chapter 1: All About Chocolate

1 Crozier, Stephen J et al., "Chocolate Seeds Are a 'Super Fruit': A Comparative Analysis of Various Fruit Powders and Products." *Chemistry Central Journal* 5, no. 1 (2011): 5.

Chapter 2: Getting Started with Cacao

1 https://www.fda.gov/Food/GuidanceRegulation/GuidanceDocumentsRegulatory Information/Allergens/ucm362880.htm.

index

Page numbers in *italics* refer to photos.

a

Almond Butter Caramel
Sauce, 40
Almond Butter Cups, 98, *99*
Almond Butter Smoothie,
Strawberry Chocolate, 54, *55*
Almond Flour and Almond
Meal, 46
Almond Joy Bars, 108, *109*
Apple Nachos, 130, *131*
avocados
Avocado Mousse with Pistachios
and Pomegranate, *200*, 201
Salted Caramel Double
Chocolate Pie, 140–41, *141*

b

"bacon," smoked, 181
baked goods. *See* desserts, baked;
morning snacks
bananas
Banana Date Cacao Smoothie,
55, 58
Brownie Trifle with Caramelized
Bananas, *138*, 139
Chocolate Banana Bread, 86, *87*
Chocolate Chip Cookie Ice
Cream Sandwiches, *208*,
209–10
Everyday Chocolate
Smoothie, 50
to freeze (prep note), 86
Frozen Bonbons, 206, *207*
Instant Soft Serve Ice Cream
with Chocolate Magic Shell,
202, *203*
Mint Chocolate Chip Smoothie,
56, 57
Morning Power Muffins, 78–79,
80–81
Zucchini Bread with Chocolate
Sweet Potato Frosting, *82*, 83
basic recipes. *See* staple recipes
Be Ballsy Energy Balls, *104*, 107

Be Saucy Chocolate Sauce, 38
Beet Lava Cakes, Chocolate,
149–50, *151*
beverages. *See* drinks
Birthday Cake, Chocolate, *146*,
147–48
Biscotti, Hazelnut Cranberry
Chocolate, 159–60, *161*
Black and White Frappe,
194, *195*
black beans, *in* Chocolate Cherry
Cookies, 164, *165*
blueberries, *in* Morning Power
Muffins, 78–79, *80–81*
Bonbons, Frozen, 206, *207*
breads. *See* morning snacks
breakfast treats. *See* morning
snacks
Brownie Trifle with Caramelized
Bananas, *138*, 139
Brownies, Fudgy You'll-Never-
Again-Want-to-Make Box,
154, *155*

c

cacao nibs
Cookies and Cream No-Churn
Ice Cream Cake, 211–12, *213*
Mint Chocolate Chip Smoothie,
56, 57
Tart Coconut Lime Pie, *142*, 143
cakes
Chocolate Beet Lava Cakes,
149–50, *151*
Chocolate Birthday Cake, *146*,
147–48
Cookies and Cream No-Churn
Ice Cream Cake, 211–12, *213*
PBH Chocolate Cupcakes,
152–53, *153*
Whoopie Pies, *176*, 177
candies
Almond Butter Cups, 98, *99*
Almond Joy Bars, 108, *109*
Be Ballsy Energy Balls, *104*, 107

Cashew Caramel Clusters,
110–11, *111*
Chocolate Bark with Fresh
Pomegranate Seeds, 124, *125*
Cookie Dough Bites, *104*, 105
Crunchy Rice Bark with Sea
Salt, *122*, 123
Dark Chocolate Fudge, 120, *121*
Favorite Freezer Chocolate
Bar, 35
Fudgy Coconut Butter
Chocolate Bar, 36
Healthy Snickers, 101–2, *103*
Homemade Chocolate Bars
Three Ways, 34–36, *39*
Mocha Chocolate Bark, *126*, 127
No-Bake Thin Mints, 114–15, *115*
Pomegranate Truffles, *104*, 106
Salted Seed and Crispy Rice
Bars, *116*, 117–18
Samoas Bars, 112–13
Traditional Raw Chocolate
Bar, 34
White Chocolate Fudge, 119, *121*
White Chocolate Peanut Butter
Cups, *99*, 100
caramel
Almond Butter Caramel
Sauce, 40
Apple Nachos, 130, *131*
Cashew Caramel Clusters,
110–11, *111*
Chocolate Caramel Popcorn,
178–79, *179*
Coconut Caramel Sauce, 41
Healthy Snickers, 101–2, *103*
Salted Caramel Double
Chocolate Pie, 140–41, *141*
Samoas Bars, 112–13
Caramelized Bananas, Brownie
Trifle with, *138*, 139
Cashew Caramel Clusters,
110–11, *111*
Cashew Milk, Mexican Chocolate,
62, 63

Cheesecake Bites, Pumpkin, *132*, 133–34
cherries
 Chocolate Cherry Cookies, 164, *165*
 Everyday Chocolate Smoothie, 50
Chia Eggs (egg replacer), 47
Chia Oatmeal, No-Cook Chocolate, *76, 77*
chocolate
 cacao versus cocoa, 20–21
 health benefits, 15–16
 history and production, 16–21
 to purchase, 23–28
 recipes, ingredients and equipment for, 28–31
Chocolate . . . (*recipe titles beginning with*). *See specific type of treat*
chocolate chips or chunks
 Chocolate Chip Cookie Ice Cream Sandwiches, *208*, 209–10
 Chocolatey Orange Scones, *88*, 89
 Cookie Dough Bites, *104*, 105
 Golden Milk Ice Cream with Chocolate Chips, 204–5, *205*
 Watermelon and Chocolate Seed Pops, *214*, 215
Chocolatey Orange Scones, *88*, 89
Churro Waffles with Chocolate Dipping Sauce, *84*, 93–94, *95*
Coconut Butter Chocolate Bar, Fudgy, 36
Coconut Caramel Sauce, 41
Coconut Lime Pie, Tart, *142*, 143
coconut shreds or flakes
 Almond Joy Bars, 108, *109*
 Chocolate Malted Milkshake, 51
 Chocolate Tart with Mashed Raspberries and Pine Nut Crust, 186–87, *187*
 Chocolate-Dipped Coconut Macaroons, *162*, 163

Pineapple "Doughnuts," *180*, 181–82
Pumpkin Cheesecake Bites, *132*, 133–34
Samoas Bars, 112–13
smoked "bacon," 181
White Chocolate Smoothie, 53
Coffee Mocha Smoothie, 59
Cookie Dough Bites, *104*, 105
cookies
 Chocolate Cherry Cookies, 164, *165*
 Chocolate Chip Cookie Ice Cream Sandwiches, *208*, 209–10
 Chocolate-Dipped Coconut Macaroons, *162*, 163
 Dulce de Leche Sandwich Cookies, 169–70, *171*
 Fudgy You'll-Never-Again-Want-to-Make Box Brownies, 154, *155*
 graham crackers, 167
 Hazelnut Cranberry Chocolate Biscotti, 159–60, *161*
 Peanut Butter & Jelly Sandwich Cookies, 174, *175*
 Sesame Crackle Cookies, *156*, 157–58
 Sugar Cookies with Chocolate Spread, *172*, 173
 Whoopie Pies, *176*, 177
Cookies and Cream No-Churn Ice Cream Cake, 211–12, *213*
Cranberry Hazelnut Chocolate Biscotti, 159–60, *161*
Creamy Homemade Nut Milks, 43
Crunchy Rice Bark with Sea Salt, *122*, 123
Crunchy Salty Peanut Butter Chocolate Tart, *188*, 189
Cupcakes, PBH Chocolate, 152–53, *153*

d
Dark Chocolate Fudge, 120, *121*
desserts, baked

Chocolate Beet Lava Cakes, 149–50, *151*
Chocolate Birthday Cake, *146*, 147–48
Chocolate Caramel Popcorn, 178–79, *179*
Chocolate Cherry Cookies, 164, *165*
Chocolate Chip Cookie Ice Cream Sandwiches, *208*, 209–10
Chocolate Cream Pie, 190, *191*
Chocolate Tart with Mashed Raspberries and Pine Nut Crust, 186–87, *187*
Chocolate-Dipped Coconut Macaroons, *162*, 163
Crunchy Salty Peanut Butter Chocolate Tart, *188*, 189
Dulce de Leche Sandwich Cookies, 169–70, *171*
Fudgy You'll-Never-Again-Want-to-Make Box Brownies, 154, *155*
graham crackers, 167
Hazelnut Cranberry Chocolate Biscotti, 159–60, *161*
Indoor S'mores, *166*, 167–68
PBH Chocolate Cupcakes, 152–53, *153*
Peanut Butter & Jelly Sandwich Cookies, 174, *175*
Pineapple "Doughnuts," *180*, 181–82
Sesame Crackle Cookies, *156*, 157–58
Sugar Cookies with Chocolate Spread, *172*, 173
Tiramisu, 183–84, *185*
Whoopie Pies, *176*, 177
desserts, raw
 Apple Nachos, 130, *131*
 Brownie Trifle with Caramelized Bananas, *138*, 139
 Pot de Crème, 136, *137*
 Pumpkin Cheesecake Bites, *132*, 133–34

Salted Caramel Double
    Chocolate Pie, 140–41, *141*
Tart Coconut Lime Pie,
    142, 143
Truffle Pudding, 135
Doughnut Holes, Chocolate-
    Glazed, 90–91, *91*
Doughnuts, Maple-Glazed
    Chocolate, 74, *75*
"Doughnuts," Pineapple, *180,*
    181–82
drinks
    Banana Date Cacao Smoothie,
        55, 58
    Be Cozy, 70, *71*
    Black and White Frappe,
        194, *195*
    Chocolate Malted Milkshake, 51
    Coffee Mocha Smoothie, 59
    Everyday Chocolate
        Smoothie, 50
    Mexican Chocolate Cashew
        Milk, *62, 63*
    Mint Chocolate Chip Smoothie,
        56, *57*
    Strawberry Chocolate Almond
        Butter Smoothie, 54, *55*
    Summer Chocolate Horchata,
        60, *61*
    Superfood Hot Chocolate,
        65, *69*
    White Chocolate Smoothie, 53
    White Hot Chocolate, 66, *67*
Dulce de Leche Sandwich
    Cookies, 169–70, *171*

e
Egg Replacers, Plant-Based, 47
Energy Balls, Be Ballsy, *104, 107*
Everyday Chocolate Smoothie, 50

f
Favorite Freezer Chocolate
    Bar, 35
Flax Eggs (egg replacer), 47
Flours, Homemade Nut and
    Grain, 46
Frappe, Black and White, 194, *195*

Freezer Chocolate Bar,
    Favorite, 35
frostings and glazes
    chocolate frosting, 148
    chocolate glaze, 90
    chocolate sweet potato frosting,
        82, 83
    maple glaze, 74
    peanut butter frosting, 152
frozen treats
    Avocado Mousse with Pistachios
        and Pomegranate (popsicle
        variation), 200, *201*
    Black and White Frappe
        (popsicle variation), 194, *195*
    Chocolate Chip Cookie Ice
        Cream Sandwiches, *208,*
        209–10
    Cookies and Cream No-Churn
        Ice Cream Cake, 211–12, *213*
    Frozen Bonbons, 206, *207*
    Fudgesicles, 198, *199*
    Golden Milk Ice Cream with
        Chocolate Chips, 204–5, *205*
    Instant Soft Serve Ice Cream
        with Chocolate Magic Shell,
        202, *203*
    Peanut Butter and Strawberry
        Ice Cube Tray Chocolates,
        196, 197
    Watermelon and Chocolate
        Seed Pops, *214, 215*
Fudge, Dark Chocolate,
    120, *121*
Fudge, White Chocolate, 119, *121*
Fudgesicles, 198, *199*
Fudgy Coconut Butter Chocolate
    Bar, 36
Fudgy You'll-Never-Again-Want-
    to-Make Box Brownies,
    154, *155*

g
Golden Milk Ice Cream with
    Chocolate Chips, 204–5, *205*
graham crackers, 167
Grain and Nut Flours,
    Homemade, 46

h
Hazelnut Cranberry Chocolate
    Biscotti, 159–60, *161*
Healthy Snickers, 101–2, *103*
Homemade Chocolate Bars Three
    Ways, 34–36, *39*
Homemade Nut and Grain
    Flours, 46
Homemade Nut Milks,
    Creamy, 43
Horchata, Summer Chocolate,
    60, *61*
Hot Chocolate, Superfood, 65, *69*
Hot Chocolate, White, 66, *67*

i
ice cream
    Chocolate Chip Cookie Ice
        Cream Sandwiches, *208,*
        209–10
    Cookies and Cream No-Churn
        Ice Cream Cake, 211–12, *213*
    Golden Milk Ice Cream with
        Chocolate Chips, 204–5, *205*
    Instant Soft Serve Ice Cream
        with Chocolate Magic Shell,
        202, *203*
Indoor S'mores, *166,* 167–68
Instant Soft Serve Ice Cream with
    Chocolate Magic Shell,
    202, *203*

l
Lava Cakes, Chocolate Beet,
    149 50, *151*
Lime Pie, Tart Coconut, *142,* 143

m
Macaroons, Chocolate-Dipped
    Coconut, *162, 163*
Magic Shell, Chocolate, 37
Malted Milkshake, Chocolate, 51
Maple-Glazed Chocolate
    Doughnuts, 74, *75*
marshmallow cream, 167
mascarpone, 183
Mexican Chocolate Cashew Milk,
    62, 63

Milks, Creamy Homemade Nut, 43

milkshakes. *See* smoothies and shakes

Mint Chocolate Chip Smoothie, 56, *57*

Mints, No-Bake Thin, 114–15, *115*

Mocha Chocolate Bark, *126*, 127

Mocha Coffee Smoothie, 59

morning snacks
Chocolate Banana Bread, 86, *87*
Chocolate-Glazed Doughnut Holes, 90–91, *91*
Chocolatey Orange Scones, *88*, 89
Churro Waffles with Chocolate Dipping Sauce, *84*, 93–94, *95*
Maple-Glazed Chocolate Doughnuts, 74, *75*
Morning Power Muffins, 78–79, *80–81*
No-Cook Chocolate Chia Oatmeal, *76*, 77
Zucchini Bread with Chocolate Sweet Potato Frosting, *82*, 83

Mousse, Avocado, with Pistachios and Pomegranate, *200*, 201

Muffins, Morning Power, 78–79, *80–81*

n

Nachos, Apple, 130, *131*

No-Bake Thin Mints, 114–15, *115*

No-Cook Chocolate Chia Oatmeal, *76*, 77

Nut and Grain Flours, Homemade, 46

Nut Milks, Creamy Homemade, 43

o

Oat Flour, 46

Oatmeal, No-Cook Chocolate Chia, *76*, 77

Orange Scones, Chocolatey, *88*, 89

Original Chocolate Spread, 42

p

peanut butter
Crunchy Salty Peanut Butter Chocolate Tart, *188*, 189
Instant Soft Serve Ice Cream with Chocolate Magic Shell, 202, *203*
PBH Chocolate Cupcakes, 152–53, *153*
Peanut Butter & Jelly Sandwich Cookies, 174, *175*
Peanut Butter and Strawberry Ice Cube Tray Chocolates, *196*, 197
White Chocolate Peanut Butter Cups, 99, 100

pies and tarts
Chocolate Cream Pie, 190, *191*
Chocolate Tart with Mashed Raspberries and Pine Nut Crust, 186–87, *187*
Crunchy Salty Peanut Butter Chocolate Tart, *188*, 189
Salted Caramel Double Chocolate Pie, 140–41, *141*
Tart Coconut Lime Pie, *142*, 143
Pine Nut Crust, Chocolate Tart with Mashed Raspberries and, 186–87, *187*
Pineapple "Doughnuts," 180, *181–82*

Pistachios and Pomegranate, Avocado Mousse with, *200*, 201

Plant-Based Egg Replacers, 47

Pomegranate and Pistachios, Avocado Mousse with, *200*, 201

Pomegranate Seeds, Fresh, Chocolate Bark with, 124, *125*

Pomegranate Truffles, *104*, 106

Popcorn, Chocolate Caramel, 178–79, *179*

popsicles
Avocado Mousse with Pistachios and Pomegranate (prep note), *200*, 201
Black and White Frappe (prep note), 194, *195*
Fudgesicles, 198, *199*
Watermelon and Chocolate Seed Pops, *214*, 215

Pot de Crème, 136, *137*

Pumpkin Cheesecake Bites, *132*, 133–34

r

raspberries
Chocolate Tart with Mashed Raspberries and Pine Nut Crust, 186–87, *187*
Instant Soft Serve Ice Cream with Chocolate Magic Shell, 202, *203*

raw candies. *See* candies

Raw Chocolate Bar, Traditional, 34

raw desserts. *See* desserts, raw

Rice Bark with Sea Salt, Crunchy, *122*, 123

Rice Bars, Crispy, Salted Seed and, *116*, 117–18

s

Salted Caramel Double Chocolate Pie, 140–41, *141*

Salted Seed and Crispy Rice Bars, *116*, 117–18

Samoas Bars, 112–13

sauces and toppings. *See also* frostings and glazes
Almond Butter Caramel Sauce, 40
Be Saucy Chocolate Sauce, 38
chocolate dipping sauce, 93
Chocolate Magic Shell, 37
Coconut Caramel Sauce, 41
Coconut Whipped Cream, 44, *45*
Original Chocolate Spread, 42

Scones, Chocolatey Orange, *88*, 89

Seed and Crispy Rice Bars, Salted, *116*, 117–18

seed-based egg replacers, 47

Sesame Crackle Cookies, 156, *157–58*

Shell, Chocolate Magic, 37
smoothies and shakes
    Banana Date Cacao Smoothie,
        55, 58
    Black and White Frappe,
        194, *195*
    Chocolate Malted Milkshake, 51
    Coffee Mocha Smoothie, 59
    Everyday Chocolate
        Smoothie, 50
    Mint Chocolate Chip Smoothie,
        56, 57
    Strawberry Chocolate Almond
        Butter Smoothie, 54, 55
    White Chocolate Smoothie, 53
Snickers, Healthy, 101–2, *103*
Soft Serve Ice Cream, Instant,
    with Chocolate Magic Shell,
    202, *203*
Spread, Original Chocolate, 42
staple recipes
    Almond Butter Caramel
        Sauce, 40
    Almond Flour and Almond
        Meal, 46
    Be Saucy Chocolate
        Sauce, 38
    Chia Eggs, 47
    Chocolate Magic Shell, 37
    Coconut Caramel Sauce, 41
    Coconut Whipped Cream,
        44, *45*
    Creamy Homemade Nut
        Milks, 43

Favorite Freezer Chocolate
    Bar, 35
Flax Eggs, 47
Fudgy Coconut Butter
    Chocolate Bar, 36
Homemade Chocolate Bars
    Three Ways, 34–36, *39*
Homemade Nut and Grain
    Flours, 46
Oat Flour, 46
Original Chocolate Spread, 42
Plant-Based Egg Replacers, 47
Traditional Raw Chocolate Bar, 34
strawberries
    Frozen Bonbons, 206, *207*
    Peanut Butter and Strawberry
        Ice Cube Tray Chocolates,
        196, 197
    Strawberry Chocolate Almond
        Butter Smoothie, 54, 55
    Watermelon and Chocolate
        Seed Pops, *214*, 215
Sugar Cookies with Chocolate
    Spread, *172*, 173
Summer Chocolate Horchata,
    60, *61*
Superfood Hot Chocolate, 65, 69
Sweet Potato Frosting, Chocolate,
    Zucchini Bread with, *82*, 83

t
tahini
    Salted Seed and Crispy Rice
        Bars, 116, 117–18

Sesame Crackle Cookies, 156,
    157–58
Tart Coconut Lime Pie,
    142, 143
tarts. *See* pies and tarts
Thin Mints, No-Bake, 114–15, *115*
Tiramisu, 183–84, *185*
Traditional Raw Chocolate Bar, 34
Trifle, Brownie, with Caramelized
    Bananas, *138*, 139
Truffle Pudding, 135
Truffles, Pomegranate,
    104, 106

w
Waffles, Churro, with Chocolate
    Dipping Sauce, *84*,
    93–94, *95*
Watermelon and Chocolate Seed
    Pops, *214*, 215
Whipped Cream, Coconut,
    44, *45*
White Chocolate Fudge,
    119, *121*
White Chocolate Peanut Butter
    Cups, 99, 100
White Chocolate Smoothie, 53
White Hot Chocolate,
    66, *67*
Whoopie Pies, *176*, 177

z
Zucchini Bread with Chocolate
    Sweet Potato Frosting, *82*, 83

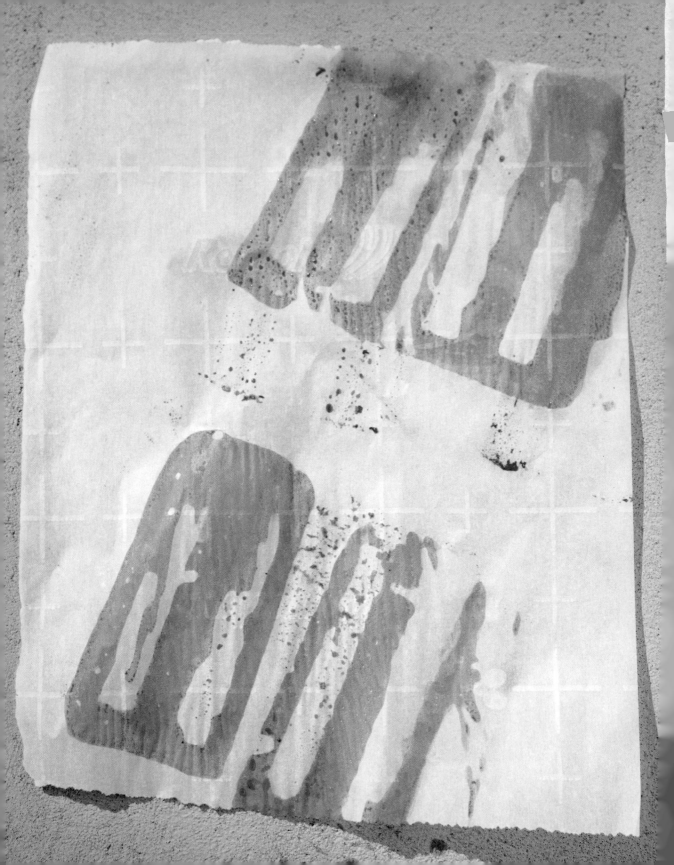